PENGUIN MODERN POETS 27

John Ormond was born in Dunvant, near Swansea, in 1923. He was educated at Swansea Grammar School and at the University of Wales. His early work appeared in *Indications* (1943) but he did not collect his poems again for a long time. For twelve years – including four as a staff writer on *Picture Post* – he was a journalist. In 1957, after a period as a producer in television news, he became a writer and producer of documentary films for the BBC. He has given many public readings in both Britain and the USA and in 1975 received the Cholmondeley Award for Poetry. In this volume he is represented by an arrangement of poems from *Requiem and Celebration* (1969), *Definition of a Waterfall* (1973), and from later and hitherto uncollected work.

Emyr Humphreys was born in 1919 and went to Aberystwyth and Bangor Colleges, University of Wales. A teacher for five years, he later became a BBC television and radio drama producer (1955–63), and then went on to start a drama department at University College of North Wales, Bangor (1965–72). He is now a freelance writer. He has published a number of novels, a novel and a play in Welsh, plus a book of poetry, *Ancestor Worship*. In 1953 he won the Somerset Maugham Award for *Hear and Forgive*, and in 1959 the Hawthornden Prize for *The Toy Epic*. He was the Gregynog Fellow in 1975.

John Tripp was born in Bargoed, Glamorgan, in 1927, and worked in journalism in London. He is now a freelance writer and literary editor of *Planet*, and lives in Cardiff. His collections of poetry are *Diesel to Yesterday* (1966), *The Loss of Ancestry* (1969), *The Province of Belief* (1971), *Bute Park* (1972) and *The Inheritance File* (1974).

Penguin Modern Poets

—— 27 ——

JOHN ORMOND

EMYR HUMPHREYS

JOHN TRIPP

Barbara & Richard
with all good
wishes from
John Ormond

Penguin Books

Penguin Books Ltd, Harmondsworth, Middlesex, England
Penguin Books, 625 Madison Avenue, New York, New York 10022, U.S.A.
Penguin Books Australia Ltd, Ringwood, Victoria, Australia
Penguin Books Canada Ltd, 2801 John Street, Markham, Ontario, Canada L3R 1B4
Penguin Books (N.Z.) Ltd, 182–190 Wairau Road, Auckland 10, New Zealand

—

This selection first published 1979

—

Made and printed in Great Britain by
Hazell Watson & Viney Ltd, Aylesbury, Bucks
Set in Monotype Garamond

Acknowledgements

For the poems by John Ormond from *Requiem and Celebration*, 1969, grateful acknowledgement is made to Christopher Davies (Wales) Ltd; for the poems from *Definition of a Waterfall*, 1973, grateful acknowledgement is made to Oxford University Press; and for the remaining poems grateful acknowledgement is made to the editors of the following magazines and anthologies: *Anglo-Welsh Review*, *Aquarius*, *Mandeville Press Spring Collection 1977*, *New Poems 1974* and *New Poems 1976–77* (Hutchinson), *Poetry Book Society Christmas Supplement 1975*, *Poetry*, *Poetry Dimension*, *Poetry Wales* and *The Times Literary Supplement*.

For the poems by Emyr Humphreys from *Ancestor Worship*, 1970, grateful acknowledgement is made to Gwasg Gee; for the poem 'An Old Man Complaining' from *Poems*, 1971, grateful acknowledgement is made to Gwasg Gomer; for the unpublished poem 'Actors X and Y' grateful acknowledgement is made to the author; for the remaining poems grateful acknowledgement is made to the editors of the following magazines: *Aquarius*, *Mabon*, *Poetry Wales*, *second aeon* and *Transatlantic Review*.

For the poem 'Dismissal' by John Tripp from *Poems*, 1973, grateful acknowledgement is made to Gwasg Gomer; for the unpublished poems 'Thin Red Line' and 'Night Sorting in Victoria' grateful acknowledgement is made to the author; for the remaining poems grateful acknowledgement is made to the editors of the following magazines: *Anglo-Welsh Review*, *Planet*, *Poetry Wales*, *second aeon* and *Transatlantic Review*.

Contents

CONTENTS

CONTENTS

JOHN ORMOND

My Dusty Kinsfolk

My dusty kinsfolk in the hill
Screwed up in elm, when you were dead
We tucked you though your hands were still
In the best blanket from your bed
As though you dozed and might in stirring
Push off some light shroud you were wearing.

We did it against double cold,
Cold of your deaths and our own.
We placed you where a vein of coal
Can still be seen when graves are open.
The Dunvant seam spreads fingers in
The churchyard under Penybryn.

And so you lie, my fellow villagers,
In ones and twos and families
Dead behind Ebenezer. Jamjars
Carry flowers for you, but the trees
Put down their roots to you as surely as
Your breath was not, and was, and was.

Early and lately dead, each one
Of you haunts me. Continue
To tenant the air where I walk in the sun
Beyond the shadow of yew.
I speak these words to you, my kin
And friends, in requiem and celebration.

Where Home Was

Home was where the glacier long ago
Gouged out the valley; where here
And there the valley's sides cohered
At bridges that had no grace.
They looked the work of men whose blunt
Belief was that a builder's guess,
If good, was better than a long
And bungled calculation.

They clamped together the two halves
Of our village, latchets of smooth
Sandstone coupling the hills.
We lived by one of them, a dingy
Ochre hasp over the branch railway.
Nearby the sidings stretched in smells
Of new pit-props leaking gold glue.
Of smoke and wild chives.

On Sundays when no trains ran
Overnight rain would rust the rails
Except, of course, under the bridges.
We put brown pennies on the silver
Sheltered lines for flattening.
Under our bridge we searched a box
Marked *Private*. In it were oily
Rags, a lantern, an oil-can.

All down the valley the bridges vaulted
The track, mortised and clasped
Good grazing fields to one where the land
Widened and farms straddled the way.
These small frustrated tunnels

Minutely muffled long strands
Of percussive trucks that clanked
In iron staccato under them.

We'd sit on parapets, briefly bandaged
By smoke. The trains went by to town.
We waved our caps to people we'd never
Know. Now it is always Sunday. Weeds
Speed down the line. The bridges
Stand there yet, joists over a green
Nothing. Easier to let them stand
Than ever to pull them down.

My Grandfather and his Apple-tree

Life sometimes held such sweetness for him
As to engender guilt. From the night vein he'd come,
From working in water wrestling the coal,
Up the pit slant. Every morning hit him
Like a journey of trams between the eyes;
A wild and drinking farmboy sobered by love
Of a miller's daughter and a whitewashed cottage
Suddenly to pay rent for. So he'd left the farm
For dark under the fields six days a week
With mandrel and shovel and different stalls.
All light was beckoning. Soon his hands
Untangled a brown garden into neat greens.

There was an apple-tree he limed, made sturdy;
The fruit was sweet and crisp upon the tongue
Until it budded temptation in his mouth.
Now he had given up whistling on Sundays,
Attended prayer-meetings, added a concordance
To his wedding Bible and ten children
To the village population. He nudged the line,
Clean-pinafored and collared, glazed with soap,
Every seventh day of rest in Ebenezer;
Shaved on a Saturday night to escape the devil.

The sweetness of the apples worried him.
He took a branch of cooker from a neighbour
When he became a deacon, wanting
The best of both his worlds. Clay from the colliery
He thumbed about the bole one afternoon
Grafting the sour to sweetness, bound up
The bleeding white of junction with broad strips
Of working flannel-shirt and belly-bands

To join the two in union. For a time
After the wound healed the sweetness held,
The balance tilted towards an old delight.

But in the time that I remember him
(His wife had long since died, I never saw her)
The sour half took over. Every single apple
Grew – across twenty Augusts – bitter as wormwood.
He'd sit under the box-tree, his pink gums
(Between the white moustache and goatee beard)
Grinding thin slices that his jack-knife cut,
Sucking for sweetness vainly. It had gone,
Gone. I heard him mutter
Quiet Welsh oaths as he spat the gall-juice
Into the seeding onion-bed, watched him toss
The big core into the spreading nettles.

Organist

Sole village master of the yellowing manual,
And market gardener: his sense of perfect pitch
Took in the cracks between the keys.
He was equipped to hear the tiny discord struck
By any weed which innocently mistook
His garden for a place to grow in.

Five days a week John Owen dug and planted,
Potted and weeded, worried
About Saturday's price in Swansea Market
For his green co-productions with God.

Walking to town at dawn, five miles
With Mary Ann his wife fluting beside him
(She, as they said, would laugh at her own shadow)
With creaking baskets laden, he nearly deafened
Himself with the noise of his own boots.

Sabbath inside the spade-sharp starch
Of his crippling collar he husbanded
On the harmonium aged couplers
And celestes into a grave, reluctant
Order; took no heed in the hymns
Of the congregation trailing a phrase behind,
Being intent and lost in the absolute beat.

But, with the years, philosopher as he was,
A Benthamite of music, he set more store
By the greatest harmony of the greatest number.
When, pentecostal, guilts were flung away
Fortissimo from pinnacles of fervour,
When all were cleansed of sin in wild

Inaccurate crescendoes of Calvary,
Uncaring, born again, dazzled by diadems
In words of a Jerusalem beyond their lives,
The choristers would stray from the safe fold
Of the true notes. John Owen would transpose
By half a tone in the middle of the hymn
To disguise the collective error,
But sure of the keys of his own kingdom.

He lies long since in counterpoint
With a few stones of earth; is beyond any doubt
The one angel of the village cloud
Who sings from old notation;
The only gardener there whose cocked ear
Can discern the transgression, the trespass
Of a weed into the holy fields,
If there are weeds in heaven.

Johnny Randall

When the moon was full (my uncle said)
Lunatic Johnny Randall read
The Scriptures in the dead of night
Not in bed by candlelight
But in the field in the silver glow
Across the lane from Howells Row;
And not to himself but to the sheep
With the village barely fallen asleep
And colliers who'd worked two-till-ten
In no fit shape to shout *Amen*
Grumbled *The bugger's off again.*

He'd dip in Chronicles and Kings
Dig into Micah, Obadiah,
Lamentations, Jeremiah,
Ezekiel, Daniel, on and on
Into the Song of Solomon:
A great insomniac heaven-sent
Digest of the Old Testament,
Faltering only in his loud
Recital when a pagan cloud
Darkened the Christian moon and bright
Star congregation of the night.

Then Johnny Randall in a vexed
Improvisation of the text
Would fill in with a few begats
Of Moabs and Jehoshaphats
(Windows banged shut like rifle-shots)
And Azels, Azrikans and all
The genealogy of Saul,

Till David's line put out new shoots
That never sprang from royal roots
And wombs long-barren issued at
The angel seed of Johnny's shouts.

When clouds veered off the moon's clean rim,
Another chapter. Then a hymn
To close the service. So he'd sing

In the big deeps and troughs of sin
No one lifts up my drowning head
Except my bridegroom Jesus Christ
Who on the Cross was crucified . . .

Then silence. Benediction: *May*
The Love of God and
The Fellowship of the Holy Spirit
Be with you always
Till the great white moon comes again.

Stillness. Until at last
Johnny would rouse himself
And take up collection from the cows.

Full-length Portrait of a Short Man

A good fat sheep, unsheared, could have bolted
Between Will Bando's legs. They made such a hoop,
Clipping his hips to the ground,
I thought he'd been a jockey. He had the gait,
The boy's body. He strutted with careful
Nonchalance, past the five village shops
We somehow called The Square, on the outside
Edges of his hand-stitched boots, punishing
The bracket of his thigh with a stripped twig.
But he'd have slipped round on a horse
Like a loose saddle-band.

                   In fact, he'd been a tailor;
From boyhood sat so long cross-legged,
Picking, re-picking his needle as though piercing
Points of dust, his sewing hand conducting
The diminishing slow movement of silko into seam,
That his legs bent and stayed bent. His years were spent
Coaxing smooth drapes for praying shoulders
Humbled on soft-named farms, stitching Sunday-best
For the small Atlases who, six days every week,
Held up the owners' world in the colliery's
Wet headings. His box-pleats in black serge adorned
The preacher proffering the great reward.

Will Bando ate perpetual cold meat
At his life's table: doomed bachelor, burdened
With thirst as might have burned his natural
Good grace; though drink increased his courtesy.
He'd tip his hat twice to the same lady,
Apologize to walls he fell against,
Pat on the head short bushes that he brushed by.

The needle's eye of village approbation
Was wide to this certain thread. But drunk,
On a dark night, his welcome was a door locked
Early against him by his lank and grudging sister.
He'd doss down in the woodshed on clean sticks.

One Sunday, deep in the thrust of red weather
Wounding October, Will was in no rick or woodshed
We could find. He'd strayed before. But Monday came
And our feet snagged paths in the morning cambric
Of frost on field after field. Every hedge and dingle
Beaten, every crony questioned, gave echoes back
As answers. Days drifted him away. In vain we cried
Into the last derelict barn, hamlets, hills distant.
The evening paper in the market town
Printed our picture silently shouting;
And one of Will from an old snapshot with a stranger's
Smile badly re-touched to a false line.

       Children at fox and hounds found him.
He lay in the broken air-shaft, twenty years disused,
Of the shut and festering pit, not half a mile
From home. Rubble and tumbled bricks
Gave him his sanctuary. Fallen where an unended
Dream of shelter brought him, he had given death
'Good evening'. His hat with orange feather
At the brim was in his hand. He wore his smart
Fawn herring-bone with the saddle-stitch lapels.

At his Father's Grave

Here lies a shoe-maker whose knife and hammer
Fell idle at the height of summer,
Who was not missed so much as when the rain
Of winter brought him back to mind again.

He was no preacher but his working text
Was *See all dry this winter and the next*.
Stand still. Remember his two hands, his laugh,
His craftsmanship. They are his epitaph.

Tombstones

Inscriptions, ritual statements
Of time's imbalance, of resources
Drained from the bank of seasons,
Painfully tell us nothing. In due course
The stonemason's phraseology will tap
Its short syllables into the skull.

Could you spell out
At death's precise dictation
A three-line version of your own life?
Could you say more in less
At half-a-crown a cut letter?

Lichens censor all but the primitive
Incisions of arbitrary dates.
Ochre elisions, encrustations
Blur the clean granite lines
Of most lives set down here.

The Key

Its teeth worked doubtfully
At the worn wards of the lock,
Argued half-heartedly
With the lock's fixed dotage.
Between them they deferred decision.
One would persist, the other
Not relent. That lock and key
Were old when Linus Yale
Himself was born. Theirs
Was an ageless argument.

The key was as long as my hand,
The ring of it the size
Of a girl's bangle. The bit
Was inches square. A grandiose key
Fit for a castle, yet our terraced
House was two rooms up, two down;
Flung there by sullen pit-owners
In a spasm of petulance, discovering
That colliers could not live
On the bare Welsh mountain:

Like any other house in the domino
Row, except that our door
Was nearly always on the latch.
Most people just walked in, with
'Anybody home?' in greeting
To the kitchen. This room
Saw paths of generations cross;
This was the place to which we all came
Back to talk by the oven, on the white
Bench. This was the home patch.

And so, if we went out, we hid
The key – though the whole village
Knew where it was – under a stone
By the front door. We lifted up
The stone, deposited the key
Neatly into its own shape
In the damp earth. There, with liquid
Metal, we could have cast,
Using that master mould,
Another key, had we had need of it.

Sometimes we'd dip a sea-gull's
Feather in oil, corkscrew it
Far into the keyhole to ease
The acrimony there. The feather, askew
In the lock, would spray black
Droplets of oil on the threshold
And dandruff of feather-barb.
The deep armoreal stiffness, tensed
Against us, stayed. We'd put away
The oil, scrub down the front step.

The others have gone for the long
Night away. The evidence of grass
Re-growing insists on it. This time
I come back to dispose of what there is.
The knack's still with me. I plunge home
The key's great stem, insinuate
Something that was myself between
The two old litigants. The key
Engages and the bolt gives to me
Some walls enclosing furniture.

The Hall of Cynddylan

after the Welsh of Llywarch Hên: 9th century

Cynddylan's hall is dark to-night,
No fire and no bed.
I weep alone, cannot be comforted.

Cynddylan's hall is all in dark to-night,
No fire, no candle-flame:
Whose love, but love of God, can keep me sane?

Cynddylan's hall is dark to-night,
No fire, no gleam of light.
Grief for Cynddylan leaves me desolate.

Cynddylan's hall, its roof is charred and dark,
Such sparkling company sheltered here.
Woe betide him whose whole lot is despair.

Cynddylan's hall, the face of beauty fallen,
He's in his grave who yesterday stood tall.
With him alive no stone fell from the wall.

Cynddylan's hall, forsaken then to-night,
So snatched from his possession.
Death take me so and show me some compassion.

Cynddylan's hall, no safety here to-night,
On Hytwyth's high expanse
No lord, no soldiery, no defence.

Cynddylan's hall is dark to-night,
No fire and no music.
My tears carve out their ravage on my cheeks.

Cynddylan's hall is dark to-night,
No fire, the company's all gone.
My tears tumble down upon its ruin.

Cynddylan's hall, to see it pierces me,
No fire, roof open to the sky:
My lord is dead and here, alive, am I.

Cynddylan's hall, burned to the very ground,
After such comradeship,
Elfan, Cynddylan, Caeawc, all asleep.

Cynddylan's hall, anguish is here to-night.
Once it was held in honour:
Dead are the men and girls who kept it so.

Cynddylan's hall, too much to bear to-night,
Its chieftain lost, O
Merciful God, what can I do?

Cynddylan's hall, the roof is charred and dark
Because the Englishry wreaked havoc on
The pasture-land of Elfan and Cynddylan.

Cynddylan's hall is dark to-night,
I mourn Cyndrwynyn's line,
Cynon, Gwiawn and Gwyn.

Cynddylan's hall, my open wound,
After the bustle, all the mirth
I knew upon this hearth.

Cathedral Builders

They climbed on sketchy ladders towards God,
With winch and pulley hoisted hewn rock into heaven,
Inhabited sky with hammers, defied gravity,
Deified stone, took up God's house to meet Him,

And came down to their suppers and small beer;
Every night slept, lay with their smelly wives,
Quarrelled and cuffed the children, lied,
Spat, sang, were happy or unhappy,

And every day took to the ladders again;
Impeded the rights of way of another summer's
Swallows, grew greyer, shakier, became less inclined
To fix a neighbour's roof of a fine evening,

Saw naves sprout arches, clerestories soar,
Cursed the loud fancy glaziers for their luck,
Somehow escaped the plague, got rheumatism,
Decided it was time to give it up,

To leave the spire to others; stood in the crowd
Well back from the vestments at the consecration,
Envied the fat bishop his warm boots,
Cocked up a squint eye and said, 'I bloody did that.'

The Ambush

after Giovanni Bellini's *The Assassination of St Peter Martyr*

Ring of black trees, late winter afternoon.
How came this bishop here in the elaborate fish-scales
Of his gold surplice, weighed down, unable to run,
Unable to flee to anywhere in the precise
Enclosing landscape, across the fields to the town
Or into the formality of the far pink hills?
Into the ring of trees wade men with swords.

The mute vermilion sun burns on their blades,
Reveals the fine, explicit, complex branches
On the horizon, every black twig exact;
With its deep falling it levers the horizon up.
The bishop and his attendants drop to their knees.
A slow light snow begins its imprecision
In this particular copse. The saints incur their wounds.
White flowers spring from the ground.

Earlier, woodcutters worked upon this spot;
Now see the tree-stumps bleed
Onto the snow with vegetable compassion
As these martyrs fall and die to rebellious men
Who make the copse a thicket with their spears.

The bloody sun's struck down. The eastern moon comes up.
In the thin beginning snow the saints
Cry out. Dusk, the still afternoon
Surrounds their cries, stifles their blood's music,
Their praise of the unfinished God.

I am the bishop, I am the men with the swords.

Design for a Tomb

Dwell in this stone who once was tenant of flesh.
Alas, lady, the phantasmagoria is over,
Your smile must come to terms with dark for ever.

Carved emblems, puff-cheeked cherubs and full vines
Buoy up your white memorial in the chapel,
Weightlessly over you who welcomed a little weight.

Lie unprotesting who often lay in the dark,
Once trembling switchback lady keep your stillness
Lest marble crack, ornate devices tumble.

Old melodies were loth to leave your limbs.
Love's deft reluctances where many murmured delight
Lost all their gay glissandi, grew thin and spare

Between a few faint notes. Your bright fever
Turned towards cold, echoed remembered sweets.
Those who for years easily climbed to your casement

Left by the bare front hall. Lust grown respectable
Waltzed slow knight's moves under the portico,
Crabbed in a black gown. You were carried out

Feet first, on your back, still, over the broad chequers.
So set up slender piers, maidenhair stone
Like green fern springing again between ivory oaks,

The four main pillars to your canopy;
And underneath it, up near the cornices,
Let in small fenestrations to catch the light.

It still chinks, spy-holing the bent laurel
With worn footholds outside your bedroom window
Through which you'd hear an early gardener's hoe

Chivvy the weeds edging the gravel path
Only to turn back into your lover's arms,
Fumblingly to doze, calling the morning false.

Lady-lust, so arranged in ornamental bed,
Baring your teeth for the first apple of heaven,
Juices and sap still run. Sleep well-remembered.

Message in a Bottle

Mariner, the persuasion of the sea
Has worked its sleight of hand again,
Again the horizon's false. So far
Your luck's held out. The sun's come up
Roughly where you expected, has swung
Clockwise in the northern hemisphere.
So far you've kept fair bearings.

But what if I say that suddenly
Beyond that horizon and its horizon too
There is no more land, that after you put out
The meridian altered, all continents fell
Away, sucked down without a blink
Of light or sigh or semaphore?
Suppose I said, 'Go sail the seas for an island,
There is none? No reef and no white water
Over coral; nothing but water, that is all your earth?'
That all your change of rigging, the fine
Rejigs to jib, genoa, spinnaker
Are vain, that all you do with the tiller
Will bring you back to nothing,
That even your departure jetty's gone,
That a slow stillness, ghost of a garden's
Fallen upon the lurching of your sea?

You'd shoot the sun again, compose yourself
With old assumptions, trust old courses
On interim charts, find reasons for the silence
On the radio, check your batteries,
Ignore the sinister becalment threatening
Your brain, curse everything before you took
New credence, believe anything rather than believe

Reality had changed, whatever reality is.
Be reassured, I'm talking to myself
And expect no one to believe me.
But it would be madness to presume
The shore you reach will not be that of a desert,
And madness, too, to suppose that the white dust there
Will not canopy into roses and then yield wheat.

Instructions to Settlers

who arrived in Patagonia from Wales, 1865

On these lean shelves of land
Nothing but thorn thrives.
At noon cross-winds foregather
To suck and subdivide
The dust and the white sand
Between one shelf and another.
With thornstumps then mark out
The plots for your bent lives.
This place is home. Possess
The wilderness with yourselves.
Dig deep. Cut down to zero,
Cut through land's wasted face
To where springs bitter with brine
Pulse sidelong and in vain
Under the restless dust,
Under the windworn plain;
And through the coarsest thorn
Strike with sharp dream, sharp bone,
To reach brief union
With this mistaken Canaan.
Search here where seed was lost,
Work stone and white to green.
Ease your tormented ghost.

Lament for a Leg

Near the yew tree under which the body of Dafydd ap Gwilym
is buried in Strata Florida, Cardiganshire, there stands a stone
with the following inscription: 'The left leg and part of the
thigh of Henry Hughes, Cooper, was cut off and interr'd here,
June 18, 1756.' Later the rest of Henry Hughes set off across
the Atlantic in search of better fortune.

A short service, to be sure,
With scarcely half a hymn they held,
Over my lost limb, suitable curtailment.
Out-of-tune notes a crow cawed
By the yew tree, and me,
My stump still tourniquéd,
Awkward on my new crutch,
Being snatched towards the snack
Of a funeral feast they made.
With seldom a dry eye, for laughter,
They jostled me over the ale
I'd cut the casks for, and the mead.
'Catch me falling under a coach',
Every voice jested, save mine,
Henry Hughes, cooper. A tasteless caper!
Soon with my only, my best, foot forward
I fled, quiet, to far America:

Where, with my two tried hands, I plied
My trade and, true, in time made good
Though grieving for Pontrhydfendigaid.
Sometimes, all at once, in my tall cups,
I'd cry in *hiraeth* for my remembered thigh
Left by the grand yew in Ystrad Fflur's
Bare ground, near the good bard.

Strangers, astonished at my high
Beer-flush, would stare, not guessing,
Above the bar-board, that I, of the starry eye,
Had one foot in the grave; thinking me,
No doubt, a drunken dolt in whom a whim
Warmed to madness, not knowing a tease
Of a Welsh worm was tickling my distant toes.

'So I bequeath my leg', I'd say and sigh,
Baffling them, 'my unexiled part, to Dafydd
The pure poet who, whole, lies near and far
From me, still pining for Morfudd's heart',
Giving him, generous to a fault
With what was no more mine to give,
Out of that curt plot, my quarter grave,
Good help, I hope. What will the great God say
At Dafydd's wild-kicking -climbing extra leg,
Jammed hard in heaven's white doorway
(I'll limp unnimble round the narrow back)
Come the quick trumpet of the Judgement Day?

JOHN ORMOND

Paraphrase for
Edwin Arlington Robinson

It was Sod's Law and not the sun
That made things come unstuck for Icarus.

The same applies to all with a seeming head
For heights, a taste for the high wires,

Flatulent aerialists who burped
At the critical moment then fell akimbo

In a tattered arc, screaming, down
Out of the illusion, the feathery Eden.

So when your mother died of black diphtheria
And neither quack nor priest would call

To give their pince-nezed ministrations,
You and your brothers wrung cold compresses

In vain for her wild brow, cleft her grave
Yourselves, thumped clods on her plank coffin.

Later one brother took to drink and drugs.
The other slotted the family investments

Into curt bankruptcy. Meanwhile your father
Tried coaxing ghosts. Table-tappings

Stuttered perniciously from the next room
To yours, harangued your shuttering deafness.

Sometime you imagined you detected clues
To a code, but it was only the singing wires

Of the death of the aural, the eighth nerve
Shrinking from lack of blood. That fenced you

High on a dangerous peak of vertigo, giddy
But unfalling. You said you mourned a 'lost

Imperial music'. What you were emperor of
Was a domain you did not recognize

As worth the name: a kingdom of aspirers
Without wings, a thin parish of prophets

Without words.— except for baffled Amen,
A scraggy choir without a common hymn,

But no man without music in the throng
And each man sawing at his own bleak tune.

Certain Questions for
Monsieur Renoir

Did you then celebrate
That grave discovered blue
With salt thrown on a fire
In honour of all blues?

I mean the dress of La Parisienne
(Humanly on the verge of the ceramic),
Blue of Delft, dream summary of blues,
Centre-piece of a fateful exhibition;

Whose dress-maker and, for that matter,
Stays-maker the critics scorned;
Who every day receives her visitors
In my country where the hard slate is blue.

She has been dead now nearly a century
Who wears that blue of smoke curling
Beyond a kiln, and blue of gentians,
Blue of lazurite, turquoise hauled

Over the blue waves, blue water, from Mount Sinai;
Clematis blue: she, Madame Henriot,
Whose papers fall to pieces in the files
In the vaults of the Registrar General.

Did you see in her garment the King of Illyria
Naming his person's flower in self-love?
And in the folds, part of polyphony
Of all colour, thunder blue,

Blue of blue slipper-clay, blue
Of the blue albatross? Blue sometimes
Without edge, blue liquified
By distance? Or did they start

Those ribbons at her wrists in blue
Of a sea-starwort? Or in verdigris, perhaps,
Blue on a Roman bead? Or in that regal blue
Of the Phœnicians, of boiled whelks;

That humbly-begun but conquering blue
Which, glowing, makes a god of man?
She who is always poised between appointments
For flirtation, what nuances of blue

Her bodice had, this blue you made
For your amusement, painter of fans and porcelain,
You set on gaiety; who saw, in the blue fog
Of the city, a candle burning blue

(Not heralding a death but) harbouring
A clear illusion, blue spot on the young salmon,
A greater blue in shadow; blue's calm
Insistence on a sense. Not for you

Indigo blue, or blue of mummy's cloth
Or the cold unction of mercury's blue ointment,
But the elect blue of love in constancy,
Blue, true blue; blue gage, blue plum,

Blue fibrils of a form, roundness
Absorbed by light, quintessence
Of blue beautiful. It was not blue
Tainted, taunted by dark. Confirm it.

The eyes are bells to blue
Inanimate pigment set alight
By gazing which was passionate.
So what is midnight to this midinette?

Ultramarine, deep-water blue?
Part of a pain and darkness never felt?
Assyrian crystal? Clouded blue malachite?

Blue of a blue dawn trusting light.

Boundaries

for Peter Tinniswood

A black flag giving assent to spring's
Illumination of the book of hours,
The whiteness of my almond tree; in anthracite
Of feathers, this blackbird singing.

Each evening just before dusk, in festival,
His pertinent cadenza to the day
Defines his territory, marks his boundary
Under my work-room window. The pane,

A yard or two of air, that's all there is
Between us. All? Yellow flute, black performer,
He flaunts his beginner's luck, chiding, gliding
Through variations upon unfound themes;

His musical unconcern crucial
To the seeming accident of song,
His obbligato signature deriving
From ancestries of whistling, unanimous

With the blossom. He, hero of branches,
(Trick of his head) perpetually surprised
To be trapped inside what he whistles,
Inventing nothing, being invention,

Flawless as makes no matter, taunting me
To delight. He essays yes out of his history
Against all configurations of silence
Through the one throat he happens to have.

Evening adjusts the trance of sky. His spate
Of acrobatics on a three-line stave,
Sardonic, repetitious, can never be whole
Except as part of what I wish to be whole.

Music to him is custom. His easy tricks
Are my despair. I turn back to the page
Where my chantepleure is born already broken.
What can I bid against him but misère?

And yet the future is still to be done.
He stabs me broad awake with notes
Not of his whistling. Thus runs spring's rigmarole
With no song substitute for any other.

Design for a Quilt

First let there be a tree, roots taking ground
In bleached and soft blue fabric.
Into the well-aired sky branches extend
Only to bend away from the turned-back
Edge of linen where day's horizons end;

Branches symmetrical, not over-flaunting
Their leaves (let ordinary swansdown
Be their lining), which in the summertime
Will lie lightly upon her, the girl
This quilt's for, this object of designing;

But such, too, when deep frosts veneer
Or winds prise at the slates above her,
Or snows lie in the yard in a black sulk,
That the embroidered cover, couched
And applied with pennants of green silk,

Will still be warm enough that should she stir
To draw a further foliage about her
The encouraged shoots will quicken
And, at her breathing, midnight's spring
Can know new season as they thicken.

Feather-stitch on every bough
A bird, one neat French-knot its eye,
To sing a silent night-long lullaby
And not disturb her or disbud her.
See that the entwining motives run

In and about themselves to bring
To bed the sheens and mossy lawns of Eden;

For I would have a perfect thing
To echo if not equal Paradise
As garden for her true temptation:

So that in future times, recalling
The pleasures of past falling, she'll bequeath it
To one or other of the line,
Bearing her name or mine,
With luck I'll help her make beneath it.

In September

Again the golden month, still
Favourite, is renewed;
Once more I'd wind it in a ring
About your finger, pledge myself
Again, my love, my shelter,
My good roof over me,
My strong wall against winter.

Be bread upon my table still
And red wine in my glass; be fire
Upon my hearth. Continue,
My true storm door, continue
To be sweet lock to my key;
Be wife to me, remain
The soft silk on my bed.

Be morning to my pillow,
Multiply my joy. Be my rare coin
For counting, my luck, my
Granary, my promising fair
Sky, my star, the meaning
Of my journey. Be, this year too,
My twelve months long desire.

Captive Unicorn

His bones are red from lady's bedstraw.
He is fed, too, according to season,
Dry meadow-rue, juiceless rest-harrow.

Enchanter's nightshade made him docile.
He was led abject, pathetic
In jewelled collar, into this palisade.

The stains on his flanks are not of blood;
The bursting pomegranates spill their seeds
From the tree where he's tethered.

He day-dreams of jack-by-the-hedge, lances
Of goldenrod to crunch on, tangled
Heart's ease, salads of nipple-wort.

His nightmares are acres of fool's parsley.
He wakes hungry for self-heal
And the clingings of traveller's joy.

Released in winter, he does not stray.
The tip of his horn a blind periscope,
He trembles in sweet dung under deep snow.

Salmon

first for, and now in memory of, Ceri Richards

The river sucks them home.
The lost past claims them.
  Beyond the headland
It gropes into the channel
Of the nameless sea.
  Off-shore they submit
To the cast, to the taste of it.
It releases them from salt,
Their thousand miles in odyssey
For spawning. It rehearsed their return
  From the beginning; now
  It clenches them like a fist.

The echo of once being here
Possesses and inclines them.
  Caught in the embrace
Of nothing that is not now,
Riding in with the tide-race,
  Not by their care,
Not by any will they know,
They turn fast to the caress
Of their only course. Sea-hazards done,
They ache towards the one world
  From which their secret
  Sprang, perpetuate

More than themselves, the ritual
Claim of the river, pointed
  Towards rut, tracing
Their passion out. Weeping philosopher,

They reaffirm the world,
   The stars by which they ran,
Now this precise place holds them
Again. They reach the churning wall
Of the brute waterfall which shed
Them young from its cauldron pool.
   A hundred times
   They lunge and strike

Against the hurdles of the rock;
Though hammering water
   Beats them back
Still their desire will not break.
They flourish, whip and kick,
   Tensile for their truth's
Sake, give to the miracle
Of their treadmill leaping
The illusion of the natural.
The present in torrential flow
   Nurtures its own
   Long undertow:

They work it, strike and streak again,
Filaments in suspense.
   The lost past shoots them
Into flight, out of their element,
In bright transilient sickle-blades
   Of light; until upon
The instant's height of their inheritance
They chance in descant over the loud
Diapasons of flood, jack out of reach
And snatch of clawing water,
   Stretch and soar
   Into easy rapids

Beyond, into half-haven, jounce over
Shelves upstream; and know no question
   But, pressed by their cold blood,
Glance through the known maze.
They unravel the thread to source
   To die at their ancestry's
Last knot, knowing no question.
They meet under hazel trees,
Are chosen, and so mate. In shallows as
The stream slides clear yet shirred
   With broken surface where
   Stones trap the creamy stars

Of air, she scoops at gravel with fine
Thrust of her exact blind tail;
   At last her lust
Gapes in a gush on her stone nest
And his held, squanderous peak
   Shudders his final hunger
On her milk; seed laid on seed
In spunk of liquid silk.
So in exhausted saraband their slack
Convulsions wind and wend galactic
   Seed in seed, a found
   World without end.

The circle's set, proportion
Stands complete, and,
   Ready for death,
Haggard they hang in aftermath
Abundance, ripe for the world's
   Rich night, the spear.
Why does this fasting fish
So haunt me? Gautama, was it this

You saw from river-bank
At Uruvela? Was this
　Your glimpse
　Of holy law?

Landscape in Dyfed

Because the sea grasped cleanly here, and there
Coaxed too unsurely until clenched strata
Resisted, an indecision of lanes resolves
This land into gestures of beckoning
Towards what is here and beyond, and both at hand.

Walk where you will, below is an estuary.
In advance to a fleeting brightness you traverse
So many shoals of the dead who have drowned
In stone, so many hibernations
Of souls, you could be in phantom country.

But the tapers of gorse burn slowly, otherwise.
And here are rock cathedrals which can be
As small as your span. And, at the water's edge,
A struck havoc of trees clutches the interim season,
The given roots bare, seeming to feed on the wind;

And in their limbs what compass of sun
Is contained, what sealed apparitions of summer,
What transfixed ambulations. If you could cut
Right to the heart and uncouple the innermost rings
Beyond those nerves you would see the structure of air.

Tricephalos

The first face spoke: Under sheep-run
And mole-mound and stifling glade
I was awake though trapped in the mask

Of dirt. Counting the centuries,
I scrutinized the void, but its question
Stared me out. What was it I remembered

As, above me in the world, generation
Upon futile generation of tall trees,
Forest after forest, grew and fell?

It was that once the ease, the lease
Of a true spring saw my brow decked
With sprigs, my gaze complete and sensual.

My eyes (the second said) were fixed
In hunger for the whole regard
Of what might be, the god beyond the god.

Time and again the black loam blazed
And shuddered with false auguries.
Passionless, vigilant, I kept faith,

Invented systems, sounds, philosophies
In which some far, long-listened-for,
Long-perfect melody might thrive.

The imagined dropped away, the perfect
Knew no advent. My sight was lost in sleep
And the stone sleep was haunted.

Two living garlands (spoke the third)
Strove to be one inside our common skull.
They half-entwined the unavailing dreams

Fashioned from light that is and words
That seemed ours for the saying.
I await wisdom wise enough to know

It will not come. The inaccessible song
Upon whose resolution we, awake, expectant,
Yearning for order, lie, is the one tune

That we were born for. Its cadence
Shapes our vision and our blindness.
The unaccountable is my stone smile.

An Ending

Lady, so long since gone, I am in limbo
Between an instinct of the dark, the sense
My own unfinished time has brought me to
And what you said you saw, and seemed to see,
On your last day. Feeling the faint pang
Of expensive appetite which, it appears,
Grates in the dying, you sent me running
For chicken and champagne. A whim, a delusion
Of hunger, that's all it was. When I returned
You saw things which I could not see.

Aren't the flowers dark? you said
Of the four yellow chrysanthemums which exploded
Pom-poms of formal light in silence
Under the black beams of that living-room
Turned sick-room; the ceiling the floor, too,
Of the empty room above in which you were born.

No one, I think now, could have invented
Such death-bed syllables. For then you said
(The poisoned, visionary words
Falling into the place of shining,
The chest of drawers, the cold brasses alive
At twitching firelight, the ticking clock
By the chimney stilled for your sleeping,
This place of much of your living
Which you had cleaned – how often? –
With cloth and polish and broom),
I can see dust on everything.

But far away you were gliding into a long beyond
Of snows, of future weather's total indifference,

Of your own uncaring. I held you in my arms
As you were dying, with no sense then of a need,
As now, which would ask, 'Why, where, these words
From one so prosaic, so afraid of any ending?'

Then you'd return with small apologies;
The sliced white chicken-breast unwanted,
The wine, in a kitchen cup to disguise
This once in a poor lifetime's last libation,
Spurned, too. Again, in shadows of shadows,
Which I believed you saw, you perceived not ease
But some uncounted-on and unaccountable
Glimpse of a pleasantness which made you say,
You who had been so afraid of your own eyes' closing
(Too easily persuaded, so I thought, of the goodness
Of this death – yet, was there someone there
Whose known gaze met your own?), *Well, well, well,*
What a surprise, what a surprise.

At last, in my arms still, those far snows
Finally kept you. The rituals done,
We stayed that night in the house together.
Neighbours fussed, grudgingly left us
Each with the other. I had no fear, mother.

And it was in my waking that I heard them,
My neighbours making up their morning fires
On either side. In the same world as them
I went down into the day that they and I would wear,
The winter sun's new garment. Into the room where you lay
I entered, took back the sheet from your face
And, without grief, grateful for your easy going,
Gave you the token of the love you were aware
No longer of, the kiss you could not share.

Forgive me for what happened then.
My lips upon your forehead tasted the foul grave
And I spat it to my hand and rushed
To wash the error from my proud flesh.

A Lost Word

In certain lights when the eyes, not seeking
Truth or effect, sometimes not even looking
Properly, see unfamiliar faces reveal
How they were long ago, young, fragile, special even,
Or predict, occupied with some thought,
Doubtless of no consequence, which ages them,
How they will look ten or twenty years hence;

And when sounds which seem on the brink
Of augury hold back, a near gale from nowhere
Dismantling the house on a cloudless summer midnight;
Or when, alone, just as coals collapse in the grate,
One hears footsteps on bare boards in the carpeted room
Above and then a voice, unanswering now, from where
It called and a shadow moved on the stairs;

One cannot escape the feeling that something
Almost at hand eludes us, that characters imprinted
On the other side of a page, in parallel, press through
On what we are trying to say, and would disclose
News or perhaps solace, some almost obvious
Simple sentence which would complete
The heart's short story of magnificence.

It would be good to believe that those strange faces
Were known once, loved maybe; that if we could find
The upstairs walkers hiding in a wardrobe
Or some cupboard and tease them from their silly shame
At being found, that stammering with surprise
At being discovered at all, or from long silence,
Unsure of their lines, they would give us the lost word.

Unable to sleep, shaving at half-dawn,
Unwilling to gaze full into the eyes
Of the latest forgery in the bathroom mirror,
Today's bad copy of an earlier work,
I have no lust for secrets. It is enough that the blade
Is sharp, that the sun lurks then rises over my garden's
Blown roses and its brown turmoil of leaves.

Homing Pigeons

Out of a parsimony of space unclenched,
Into the not known and yet familiar,
They ascend out of their hunger, venture
A few tentative arcs, donate new
Circumflexions to the order of strange sky;
Then blend to a common tangent and so render
Themselves to the essence of what they are.

What beguilement shepherds the heart home?
Not what we know but some late lode-stone
Which, far, was always there, drawing us
To a meaning irreducible, to a fixed star.

Why then the falling, all the fumbling
As tumbler pigeons, fools flying, with the most
Inept of masteries? But flying still
And, despite awkwardness, being, as best we can,
Committed, in the chance weather we approach,
To what and where, without a sense of reward,
We may reach and trust to be fed.

EMYR HUMPHREYS

THE ANCESTOR WORSHIP
CYCLE

I *Ancestor Worship*

1

The dead are horizontal and motionless
They take less room
Than the stones which mark the tomb

But the words they spoke
Grow like flowers in the cracked rock

Their ghosts move easily between words
As people move between trees
Gathering days and sunlight
Like fuel for an invisible fire.

2

Grandparents whose portraits hang
Like ikons in our hearts
Carved out acres drew up codicils
To brace our lives
But the new estates cover the fields
All the names are changed and their will
Is broken up by sewers and pylons.

3

Our remote ancestors knew better.
They were all poets
They all wove
Syllabic love into their wooden homes

They saw the first invaders come
Pushing their boats through the water meadows

Their teeth and their swords glittering in the stealthy light
And they carved metrical systems out of their own flesh.

4

The air is still committed to their speech
Their voices live in the air
Like leaves like clouds like rain
Their words call out to be spoken
Until the language dies
Until the ocean changes.

EMYR HUMPHREYS

II *Poet of the Old North*

E bore duw Sadwrn cad fawr a fu –

Saturday morning a great battle began
Blood shed as long as the day lasted

Their mouths were filled with earth
But his words were not wasted

It was more to him than a demographic swing
The barbarous thrust more than an ethnic threat
Covered with classroom notes his verbs
Are bloodstained faces.

Four hosts led by the Destroyer attacked from the east.
The warm kingdoms summoned their men, the training
                                                     feast
Was foregone. Out of the silence burst the voice of the
                                                     Blusterer
'Send your hostages forward
Send them dressed in the garments of peace
Call me Overlord call me master
And from this day our conflict shall cease . . .'

Unreproducible blunt repetitive rhymes
Like the breath in his lungs
Made short and immediate by danger
The last moment the culmination of times
Of postponement. The cold future hangs
In the air while the nation waits for the leaders' answer.

Owain son of Urien in the vanguard
Made the first reply. So proud of his descent
His voice was the first blow. 'There are no hostages

There will be none. Today or any day.'

Then his father spoke, Urien, Taliesin's master,
The great lord of the lakes, the leader of the host:

'They wish to meet us! They have proposals to discuss!
Make a fence of linked shields! Let us
Show them our faces over a rim of steel! Let them
See spears level above our heads! Let us
Fall upon them and pick out his head
From their ranks as they tumble
In heaps before us.'

And there he pauses.
No account of the battle is given
Only the scene at nightfall

Before Llwyfain wood
Between the hills the site forgotten and the country lost
The corpses have stopped bleeding
But the gorged crows are daubed with blood.

What does *armaf* mean?
Armaf arfaethu, paratoi cân?
– *virumque cano* – Push the letters about
Split the syntax, change the language

The voice of the poet fits
His cattle on the narrow bridge
Defy the passage of time

As the little scholar said
Old deaths are the latest

Take a year take a lifetime
To hammer out this song.

III *A Roman Dream*

The dust of the chariot race is in my hair.
I hide under the laurel bush like a piece of silver.
The guards use ferrets and before dawn they will find me.

Last night the Emperor painted his face green,
We all agreed this was the correct colour.
I was a little drunk. I agreed too much.

His god-like gaze discovered me,
An academic working on his uncle's prose.

I have long admired your style, he said,
But recently I find it makes the content suspect.
Come with me.

With green lips he kissed the short sword
And put it in my hands.
With green hands, he exposed the prisoner's ribs,
An unknown prisoner whose face he said
For my sake had been covered.

Here, he said smiling. Here. Between the third and fourth
                                                            ribs.

                                                    Push.

Push.

Whose was the face beneath the napkin?

Push.

I wish to be loved by all men
I have spent fifteen hours a day
On Odes to be admired

In addition to my academic work
My research
My teaching duties.

Push

My contributions to enlightened journals
On the balance of ambition and duty to the state
On the rational content of the Imperial dream
On human dignity

Push

On precision in syntax
On language truth and logic

Push

His royal hand, soft and perfumed, closed over mine
With childlike suddenness pushing

The warm blood hit my face

Sounds came from my throat like vomit

The faces of gods are green, he said not red.
Would you agree?
I nodded and I nodded.
Will you die for me?

I don't care what you choose but make the choice your own
Fall on this sword like a Roman
Or swallow poison like a talkative Greek ...

The air was cold as marble.

The green god was bored.

Or run to hiding like a rabbit and my guards will hunt
                                                    you...

If I could get to the hills
Somewhere in Tuscolo beneath my teacher's ruined villa
There is a hiding place and a secret spring.
If I could find the strength to make the journey
There is dry blood on my lips
The dust of the chariot race is in my hair.

IV An Apple Tree and a Pig

Oian a parchellan, ni hawdd cysgaf
Rhag godwrdd y galar y sydd arnof.

1

All men wait for battle and when it comes
Pass along the sword's edge their resilient thumbs.

Men clasp in faithless arms their sobbing wives
Tasting even in the salt kiss the bliss pricking points of
knives.

Men clip on armour and see in their children's eyes
Their swollen images, their godlike size.

Men assemble together, create a new sea
That floods into battle. Men become free

Of the dull bonds of life, become locked in a fight
In love in league with Death, lost in icy delight.

2

In such a frenzy I slaughtered my sister's son.
My sword cut open his face and I screamed as though I had
won

Glory to nurse in the night, until I turned and saw
The flesh of Gwenddolau, the young king who loved me,
raw

And Rhydderch's sword dull with Gewnddolau's blood
And his great mouth trumpeting joy. Ah then I understood

That rooted and nourished in my own affectionate heart
Was the spitting devil tearing our world apart.

3

When I fled to the wood, alone I lay under a tree
Still hearing the clash of our swords, still dumb in my
                                                    agony.

So much despair had crowded into my heart
My tongue was cold, speech a forgotten art.

As I lay in the wood I suffered the germ of peace
To penetrate my veins like a lethal disease.

I have lost all desire to communicate with men.
My sighs do not disturb the building wren.

An apple tree and a pig: these are my friends
With whom I share my wisdom that no longer pretends

To be wise, since nothing my wisdom brings
Can restore the lost kingdom or challenge the armour of
                                                    kings.

I have eaten the apple of knowledge and all I know
Is that love must fail and lust must overthrow

And in the nights of winter when the ice-winds howl
A pity and a terror fasten themselves on my soul

And I cry upon death to wrap his white redress
Without mercy about the stillness of the merciless
And remedy my madness with long silence.

V Dialogue in a Garden

We sit and talk like subjects of a dream
In a garden where the five senses
Float in five personifications and we remain
Sitting in deck chairs moving mouths
Moving the mouth piece of the dreaming brain.

    And you ignore the pipestem stuck between your teeth
    Tobacco smoke that blends with other smells
    The declining sun, my voice that cuts the evening air
    In this seclusion far
    From the unreality of war.

Have I not lain on a tenement roof at night
And watched the sky turn into a battleground
Death dropping from the engines in the sky
Fiercer than molten lead poured down the scaling ladder,
More mutilating than torture.
I have walked a surburban street like Abednigo in the
                             flames
And stood, alive among the flames of death.

    Yesterday I bent my back
    And thrust a sharp spade through the soil
    Ate meat and potatoes for dinner and went to bed
    Soothed with the pleasant ache of toil.

Toil . . . work is a protracted dream
Body and Mind circling in the half-conscious.
Life comes to life near death.
For many days and nights I stood
At the crude operating table seeing stripped bodies
Poised between Life and Death.

I have buried dead lambs with keen regret
Throwing earth over wool, stamping on turf
I straighten to reflect
Enrichment of the soil and future glowing sward
And look about at sheep nibbling the rising grass.

Once in a smoke screen we attacked
Threw ladders on barbed wire
Ran shouting to attack
When others dropped, bullets passed or stopped,
I ran on to achieve the trench
My bayonet reached its goal
Twisting in a foreign belly
Strange intimacy;
I remember ecstatic dying eyes seeking mine in gratitude.

It grows cold: shall we go inside?

VI Dream for a Soldier

First thing after breakfast I'll ride out
Into the spring, and the dazzling sun
Shall glitter on the sliding river, and break
Munificently through bud-broken branches
I'll ride out as innocent as the young morning
Ignorant as a wish, with no ulterior motive
And almost as though by accident we shall meet
And I shall kiss you 'good morning.'

We shall go on together. Perhaps we shall sing
Our voices blending naturally with
The cool music of an isolated thrush
And water falling among rocks.

We shall pass a blind man and two brown horses
Harrowing a stony field, and call out
'Good morning, brother.' He will smile
Without seeing us and wave with an uncertain hand.

The road will pass through a wood; a cock-pheasant
Will march like a guardsman through the tall bluebells
Onto the road, but rising at our approach
Obliquely on whirring wings.

The landscape will not be new but lovably familiar,
Hallowed by a past we cannot remember
The fallen wall, the ruin, and the incongruously leaning
                                        boulder.

As we climb dead fern shall crackle under our feet
The heavy smell of gorse in the sun shall assail us
And where we rest, clean and cropped like a lawn,
Private as a park among the rocks.

This day shall move as a symphony
No less enchanting as its end approaches,
Crossing the fields, the fence adorned
With a carrion crow and the pinned out pelt of a weazel.

The sun declines. Withdraws with enormous grace
A dumb flourish in the minor key.

We shall be unarmed and harmless as doves
As we wander slowly homeward, towards the house
Where the seven deadly sins are locked in a book
And O how beautifully tired and simple
Our prospect of rest as we stand by the window
Watching the twilight assemble

Miraculously unaware of the horror over the hill
The stricken village cold faces and hot guns the military
                                                    thunder
As we lay our unblemished heads on a common pillow
And sink like gods into a wholly selfish dreamless slumber.

VII On the Death of an Old Woman

The doctor gave her three months.
Always economical she took two.
Only daughter married, living far away,
Her life wound up, what else was there to do

Except lie still in a cottage hospital bed
Have faded visions between bouts of pain
Swallow so many teaspoonsful of gruel
And throw them up again.

Her brittle belly could hold nothing down.
The nurses fed her lightly to keep her clean,
Ate the small bunch of grapes the vicar sent her
And drank the quarter pint of cream.

Her last few days of life were rather a problem
Ethically, we considered, was she of any use
No family, no hope, a wasted body;
The question was abstruse . . .

O biblically stripped of all protection
A rotten seed sterile of further production
No power in her withered hands, breasts dry
And shrunk, a failing brain,
Belonging to no one, and by no one claimed:
The woman had no function.

Every remaining day she lived
At the community's expense
Preserved in secrecy
To avoid offence

To the thriving world outside
The lusty business of living;
To them her futile presence would have been
The scarecrow criminal hung on the windy hill.
She would have caused politicians to shudder
Soldiers to cry and film-stars to fall ill.

VIII *At the Frontier*

Six drunken soldiers at the barbed-wire frontier:
From the beer, gin, whisky, rum, churning in their bellies
Fumes swirl like incense into their heads.
They stare with bloodshot sullen eyes and blink
At our steady sober headlights. Resentfully
They call out for our passes, curse at us
For our cold intrusion. (My lights
Are the parson's book and the sexton's bell)
Fumbling around, armed and dangerous
They frighten the women and make the men uneasy.

These, we think, are six beasts, made bold
With bayonets and guns, drunk not only
With liquor but also with an illusion
Of power for life and for death.

They would willingly shoot or stab, we think,
At the slightest provocation, kick a woman's ribs
With a bully's hob-nailed boot, mutilate
A corpse with animal pleasure, view
Blood with stupid fascination
And grunt with a primaeval exultation.

We hate these men as we wait in the dark,
We resent their indecent portrayal
Of what we dream or know lies in ourselves.
An honest comrade mutters, 'There but for
The grace of God, go I,' and all are profoundly insulted,
Horribly disturbed.

I think we would view their execution
By guillotine, or chair, or rope, or bullet,

Each of us has his private preference, his *bête noir*
With a cold satisfaction or perhaps,
The more sensitive, with the vague pity we expend
On an old dog or crazy bull being shot.

At two o'clock six drunken soldiers staggered
Vomiting and cursing, off to bed, collapsing
On straw palliasses, sleeping as they fell,
Arms out or legs bent under.
Some moan like frightened children in their sleep:
One sees a childhood devil; one an enemy;
Another sees Ma in the little kitchen baking scones –
Her cracked and soapy hands on washing days;
An awkward kiss in the alley, the girl ran home –
The smell of a hay loft in autumn – the smell
Of a dung heap being turned on a frosty day –
A beaten wife's deliciously unwilling love –

Six drunken soldiers. Tomorrow morning
Comes the biliously green dawn,
The agonising yawn, the half-hearted curses.
The youngest will say, rubbing his
Stupidly wet soft mouth – 'The bloody hell I care.'

IX *The Hermit*

Everything that happens is a message:
Sleeplessness, stars out of sight, a misprint on a page,
The shape of that sack in the broken window pane.

I am fifty if you ask me but my age
Like my smell is meaningless. It measures
The air I have used, the decay in my teeth
And the walls of my hut. It is not the age of stone
Or even its strength that speaks to me:
Only its stillness.

She was never still. She wore hats
That made me laugh and scream. Naked
She made demands that turned me into a dog.

You may say I should never have married
And I would agree if it were any consequence
But it no longer matters. The night she tore my arm
And spat in my blood she gave me
The sanctity of an object the colourless varnish
That preserves from diminishing contacts the glaze
That protects my human skin while those messages
Shuttle through the day and night and transform
The sores on my hands into crystal flowers.

I am a man made free. My hut stands
In the corner of the field. The rats run in the rocks
The rooks congregate above me. My feet
Are wrapped in sacks my food is mouldy

But the foreshore is my kingdom, finding
Objects and listening to the waves I am
Collecting signals: the bones of a dead bird

A mollusc in a pool of purple water, sadness
A piece of wormeaten wood I am collating
A notation of the universe for the birth of a word
I need my solitude.

X *My Great-aunt*

My gloves ... Thank you my dear. And my spectacles of
course.
And where did I put my hymn-book? Oh dear ...
Is it February or March? March? The first Sunday in
March ...
I must sit down a moment. A silly old woman I am
Yes I am. The first Sunday in March. The unspeakable
weather
Turns mild ... this muffled rain.

Seventy five years ago my little sister died.
So long ago you may say, but it remains,
Becomes more and more as I myself walk towards death
My fiercest yesterday. A dream recurring.
A dream I never learn to understand.
A simple death. A two year old with a teapot in her fist
Tumbles into the sexton's silence, into black rain water,
And no one hears her cry. I was seven then
And it was I that missed her. But the call and the search
And the anguish came too late. Father found her;
Mud from the ploughed field on his buttoned leggings
And his sheep-dog, Mot, sneaking unnoticed across the
forbidden threshold
He carried my sister, her dripping body, irretrievably cold
Into the warm kitchen and laid her on the table
That is all I remember. They say he did this and that;
But I remember the unstirred pools about her little feet.

One year later my mother died.
My father married again. A woman called Leonora.
Rather stupid. She used to say I was never 'on her side.'
When I was twelve the family was no longer mine.
I remember these things more clearly since your uncle died.

There have been wars I know, and great disasters
A long life gains wide experience of weeping and tears.
But I have always been described as a cheerful woman.
I remember her last in her little coffin before the lid was
                                                screwed down,
Washed and so neatly dressed, her face not unduly distorted.

I myself am on the edge of death and that is what I
                                                remember
Because Time is nothing and as long as we live
We are liable to the sum of the world's sorrows at any given
                                                time.

My gloves my dear? I am wearing them you say?
And John, I mean David, taking me to Chapel in the car.
Forgive me, I keep on calling you John
My memory my dear. You know. Completely gone.
Now please don't either of you be vexed
I'm a silly old woman. Forget my own name next.

XI *Uncle Thomas*

His sermons were thick with symbols
When Elijah for instance mounted the fiery chariot
He dropped his cloak and this meant something;
When the alabaster box of ointment broke
The perfume was God's love filling the house;
A servant ploughing was more than a servant ploughing
An image always stood for something else.

His eloquence was measured.
His popularity greatest
Among middle class congregations
I know of a chemist's shop in Llandudno
Where his epigrams are still treasured.

He was a man of some standing in the denomination.
He examined candidates for ordination.

His repertoire was full of loving images
And anecdotes that reassured
He listened patiently to children's verses
And told the sick that they would soon be cured.

At home he read philosophy in bed
His wife complained he never heard what was said.

Suffering from indigestion, old age and people
He told me once he found the world absurd.

XII Mrs Jones

There's a use for something every seven years, she says.
Always gnomic, she fills the leaking coffee pot with Indian
                                                        corn
To fatten the geese that crop the orchard grass
And leave their wet droppings under the trees.

Her eyes glitter behind her spectacles
Like sunlight on a wild sickle like
The setting sun on mountain cottage windows like
Undeclared love.

A tuft of black hair waves from the mole on her chin as she
                                                        speaks
Earlier her rage struck the flagstones her clogs
Woke up the serving maids her smile
Was a kiss and a curse her single words
Put pebbles in my cream

Daily her energy drove us
Her words were whips
She managed machines and men

But today, twenty one years later her loving comes of age
It lives in this estate, this
Blossom of gorse, a sigh in the grass
As far away as horses in a field.

XIII *Gŵr y Rhos*

There is no such thing as the image of a country
For this reason put up this flag for approval:
It is made of skin and stained with sunlight and tobacco
It speaks in pickled phrases the language of apples
And it is wide enough for a shroud.

It remembers the road as a track, pigs
In every sty, a railway running, a harbour
With ships, a quarry working, fresh fish, young people
And planting trees in holes big enough
To bury a horse.

This man is a king except
He makes his living emptying caravan bins
And uses English in the shop to avoid giving offence
To visitors who do not know
Where they are or who he is.

XIV *Pastoral*

This morning, yawning, Dic Fawr said
'Evans the " *Ship and Castle* " is dead'
'Is he indeed? Poor chap,' I said.

The huge horse rose in its shadowy stall
We smoked and watched its brown excreta fall
And Dic, said, spitting 'After all

You couldn't expect a chap like that
With bottles to hand from where he sat
Not to soak. His belly was like a vat.'

Dic went across to stir the horse's feed.
'Come on, Eat up,' he said, 'you're harrowing the fifteen
                                    acre field
All day today,' and wistfully to me, 'It was a nice death
                                    indeed.'

Outside the lark was gargling with dew
When Dic led out Captain Bell and True
The sunlight dripped in the lane. The sky was blue.

XV *A Democratic Vista*

Strange sanctuary this, perched on the rising cornstack
Like a desert saint on a broken pillar
Staring, eyes unstirring until hill field sea are one
The procession of thought blurred
Into the regular rising and falling of a sinewy arm
And the dry rustle of sheaves.
Tom Williams, Guto, Dick Williams, Wil bach, Dafydd
                                        Dew and me,
We are the people; our conversation is smooth and
                                        superficial
Like a veneer of grained wood, curves leading nowhere
Which was where they started.
We are the people, for whom politicians shout and soldiers
                                        fight
We sow and reap, eat and sleep, copulate in secret, think
In circumference of one dimension.
We are the sacred people, the secular mystery, the host,
Whitman's elastic deity, Marx's material, Rousseau's noble
                                        savage
Mayakovsky's beloved –
Tom, Guto, Dic, Wil, Dafie, and me –
Reasonably efficient between dawn and sunset,
God chewing tobacco, God drinking tea, digesting rice.
We are the people.
God is not mocked.

XVI From Father to Son

There is no limit to the number of times
Your father can come to life, and he is as tender as ever he
was
And as poor, his overcoat buttoned to the throat,
His face blue from the wind that always blows in the outer
darkness
He comes towards you, hesitant,
Unwilling to intrude and yet driven at the point of love
To this encounter.

You may think
That love is all that is left of him, but when he comes
He comes with all his winters and all his wounds.
He stands shivering in the empty street,
Cold and worn like a tramp at the end of a journey
And yet a shape of unquestioning love that you
Uneasy and hesitant of the cold touch of death
Must embrace.

Then, before you can touch him
He is gone, leaving on your fingers
A little more of his weariness
A little more of his love.

XVII *Twenty-four Pairs of Socks*

In the chest of drawers there are two dozen pairs of warm
                                                    socks.

The man who wore them had the secret of living.
He was prepared at any time to say what it was
so that as far as he was concerned
it was no secret.

When he lived I could not think
that what he believed brought him peace and happiness,
was the true source of content.
If he said FAITH I remembered his ulcer.
Whether installed by heredity or induced by anxiety
an ulcer is surely something that nags,
coaxed to grow in a greenhouse of despair.

If he modestly implied GOOD WORKS by his concern for
                                                    others
and his unswerving devotion to political idealism of the
                                                    most naive kind.
I would like to point out that he never cleaned his own
                                        boots until his wife died
and as far as I know
no party he voted for or supported ever stood in danger
of being obliged to exercise power.

Sometimes his calm was unnerving.
At others, one sock of a pair missing, or some such trifle
he would tremble and then erupt, –
the burst of red-faced fury
of an angry peasant cheated at a fair.

But mostly he was calm. Nearly always.

(Not counting a certain tremolo when he was swept with
righteous indignation.)

It was generally accepted that he was a good man,
and it pleased him deeply to know that his visits were
welcomed.
In the wards his presence, his nod and bow especially,
did everyone a lot of good.

Everything about him suggested that the secret was not his
own
but something given, something to share that came from a
source outside –
available to all like the warmth of the sun and words.

He was a preacher of course.
The drawers of his desk are packed so tight with sermons
they refuse to open.
His three suits of clerical grey hang in the little wardrobe.
In the chest of drawers there are twenty four pairs of warm
socks.

XVIII *Master Plan*

He bought stones first in the corners of fields
And thorn bushes for birds

He bought time like a lotion
To smear over the island in an amber light

He bought a master plan for the reconquest of the island
In such a way that loving bodies
Would not lie in the streets in pools of blood

Across the only bridge
He threw a language barrier

In the sea he inserted prohibitive sunsets
To change the nature of the invader

Growing flowers from the stems of their guns

He bought a tomb in the rocks
And invested all that was left in the stars.

An Old Man Complaining

1

Before my back bent I was a bright talker
A story-teller an unique performer
With easy access to generous princes

Before my back bent I was handsome boasting
About my spear always first to draw blood
Now I am crookback cold croaking

Before my back bent my legs were bold
I strode into the great hall instantly included
A guest with a place of honour in Powys.

2

Listen little crutch the spring has come
A cuckoo hides to do his grieving
Not one girl needs my loving

The summer is coming wooden crutch
The furrows open the shoots are green
And you manifest my weakness

Wooden crutch I think of harvest
The fern stands red the stubble yellow
What I used to love I now use least

Wooden crutch this is winter
The warriors make merry indoors
Nobody visits my little room

Except you my mute my familiar
Stand by my unsteady tongue
Wiser a straight wand than a crooked talker

Stay by my side sustain me
Bear with me wooden brother
I am bereaved. Be hard with me.
Unmoved. Ignore my chatter.

3

Old Age is having its fun
My hair and my teeth are hidden
And you can't tell me where to find them
I envy you your erect stem
Could still impress the young

I say that swine Old Age
Has hidden my teeth and my hair
I'll keep you close to me
Women like your stem better than mine.

The wind cracks. There are white skirts
To the trees. A stag is brave. The hill bare.
I am frail. My steps very slow.

A leaf like this pushed about by the breeze.
I'll be sorry for it. Fate they call it.
Already old. Born this year.

4

All I craved for in those days I now refuse.
A young woman. A hard foe. An unbroken stallion.
Somehow they no longer suit me.

I have four servers left. I can name them.
They never fail. Infection.
Cough, Thorned Ague. Chill Old Age.

5

I am old. Alone. Ugly with cold
I once lay in a royal bed
Now I am unwarmed. Wretched.

The shape of a crook. A broken fool.
Fickle. Savage. Uncivil.
Even those left who loved me avoid me

And no girl comes by. Who would want to see me?
Not even Death
I can't go out to call him in

Or call my sons back from the grave.
Gwawr and Gwên! I can't sleep thinking about them

The night I was born
It all began
My long life is a proverb about pain.

Adapted from *Canu Llywarch Hen*

Bourgeois Nationalism

Keep away from the radio
The morning is waving at you
And the birds are blowing
Benedictions and clichés

Close the gates. The top gate and the bottom gate.
Open your eyes
To the full infectious glitter
Of wall flowers and the power of weeds

Bring the argument to a close
With the white haired English professor
Who hates the Pope
Loves the British Empire still
And worships mathematics
Stop him running about the garden
Shouting Progress Progress
And the individual doesn't matter
And it's all psychology really
Send him back to Staines

Sit under the wall
Licking the wind and the weather
Study the sycamore leaves
And those impudent spruces
Grabbing more space
Sit under the wall
And wait for the cat to speak Welsh.

The Last Exile

A royal profile sulks into a pile of pillows
Sparse hair lies passive under a net
Her eyes make claims
Her eyes are never still

Her loyal servant that plastic earpiece
Has slipped
It dangles its faint distortions
Over the side of the iron cot
Near the bell she disdains to reach

She has come to rest in the white ward
The wheeled cot is the last vehicle

There is whiteness everywhere
And listening

The room is the length and breadth of a pause
And is closing in on the jaded pattern
Of programmes processed in a distant capital
The printed circuit of her heart's desire
The flutter of purple and rustle of flowered skirts
The ordered breathing of faithful clocks

The blood has drained from her ear
Her eyes are never still

She is repairing the cracks as they appear
With moist collects fragments of creeds
Ancient alphabets
But faster than she can work now
To restore the palace of her resounding past
The white pause is contracting.

Novelette

Mr and Mrs Cavendish-Cooper
How do you do
How kind of you to come
Never spoke to each other
For thirty years
Except in the presence of a third person
Cause and effect
Like a man and wife
When left alone
Lived in a silent house.

He took all the blame
That fatal visit
Prompted by boredom
To a Brazilian brothel
And the warm confession
Her eyes that wouldn't focus
As a result.

They gave famous parties
Filling the house and garden
Until they shimmered
In an alcoholic haze
Happy with gin
He told the parson
'All my life I've got on well
With every living soul
Except my wife.

Women are strange and unreliable
You've heard the story padre
About two women in a wood
Who came across a tramp?

Property unlike woman
Is not violent
And goes up in value
You can understand my preference
My only daughter bless her
I always wanted a son
She sees her mother's side

Well now she wants to marry
And there he is. I've got him
A failed B.A.
He owns a hand-made
Pair of shoes
And he's after my estate

But never mind. We talk
I know how to handle him
Such a lovely day
Can I get you another? The same again?'

His gin-flushed face
Fell into the flower-bed
All the women screamed
Except his wife.

The Colonel and his Lady

My armed man
Decorated for slaughter
His boots I licked
They aspired to rank
They arrived
He was first to the ridge
His eye blown out
He turned and hollered
'Where the hell you bin?'

Gilded with rank
Gold in the vanguard
Before a woman still
Young and breathless
He paid in full
For the palace mead

To administer death
In another country
He left me waving
On the summer lawn
A man goes forth
To seek his fortune
With seasoned troops
With armoured cars
With tanks at his side

In his frenzy
Mercy was frozen
He came to battle
In search of blood
In the ranks left standing

He flashed like a sickle
Among the green reeds

He was first to the river
As they say he took it
His sergeant was killed
Deserters were shot
In the bright morning air
They drove over corpses

A day for assembling fine weapons and armour
A day for advancing singing shouting
A day for destruction and a day
For the counting of corpses
Sharp axes sharp swords
Sharpest of all that day
In the minds of mothers

He licked my flesh
So welcome home
My muscular god one eyed
My sweating survivor
He will buy more horses
And a new Mercedes
The General insists
He must join his club

'*At the rough ford*
My best friends fell' . . .
Weakness enters
At night without warning
A man's wide heart
On lips still living
The battle song falters

On lips still living
The taste of death

At night when I touch him
I count the stars
My armed man
Sweats in my arms
Under his pillow
His teddy-bear hides
Ready to be touched
When he cries in his sleep.

EMYR HUMPHREYS

Turkeys in Wales

Tenders are invited for the supply of turkeys to County Council
Establishments.
  Gwent County Council, September 13, 1975

Certain turkeys survive
They believe in their exemption
Attribute
Their extra days
To the music
Of their eloquence
And their influence
With the Owners.

Their cold combs
Are colourless and flaccid
Their long necks
Shredded with age
Their feet are decorated
Like their feathers
With fading orders
And birthday honours.

They consider the stony field
A sphere of influence
Or at the least
A corner of comfortable exile
Reserved for their survival.

The hungry young
Observe them
And the brightness of the seed corn
Those tireless beaks
Gobble with horny care.

Such birds
They whisper between themselves
Consume the last lumps
Of our sunlight

While comrades in fresh feathers
Are snatched
And sacrificed

If we had hands
We could learn
To turn
Necks into wreaths.

Hawkins without a Number

Hawkins. He had a lesson to provide
On the retention of urine
Toothless unshaven he slipped through
The regulations like a snatch of sound
Through a keyhole
Or a bubble in a waterpipe.

He stood in the middle of the cell
Between his cot and mine
Scratching his head and muttering
The screws. They think I'm having them on
But honest to God I don't remember see.

You say something and I take it in
And then I blink and I've forgotten it
And they don't believe me see. So what can I do about it?

I've not got half my kit. That's for sure.
Are them your own teeth mate?
I've left my set at home. I can't do nothing with them.
What time is it do you know? There aren't no
Clocks in this place then? No I've not been in before
Ah well. If I knew the time I'd forget it
So what's the use?

He has a decision left. In his clothes
With his boots on. To sleep
He has forgotten to use the pot
But he snores more beautifully
Than a pig rooting about in
A forest of fallen leaves. Hawkins.

Actors X and Y

X

Consider an actor of fifty or pushing fifty
Who is still fond of himself, who still feels
The skin of his neck with a certain affection
Who still dares to use a reasonably well-bred masculine
scent
And brushes his hair with the exact care due
To a greying veteran of histrionic wars.

Such a man has come to terms with himself
Rotating as he does on an axis of self-awareness.
Such a man has survived disappointment, insult, vilification,
Total misfortunc and a measure of success.
And in so doing he has acquired a skill at handling himself
That is akin to the power of the old-fashioned seaman,
A knowledge of navigation as refined as that of a migrating
bird.
He lives comfortably with his image.
He has lent himself to the imagination of his race
Advertising good looks, clothes, wine, tobacco, and how to
look after women:
The lines on his face are the markings of a cultivated flower.

For this reason, when he stamps and swears on a rehearsal
floor
It is easy to forgive him. When he has found his way into
the part
And made it fit him, he will be calm and content
As a child after a meal
Will easily smile to show who ever cares to watch
That he is blessed with a full stomach and an unmalicious
heart.

Y

Nothing about acting is easy: on the other hand
It requires stupidity to do it well and a certain daring;
Stupidity, that is, that animals display
When they repeat an action
With the mindless eagerness that is the source of physical
grace:

A cat for instance stretching
To the same height against a door that will never open
Or an ewe turning to stamp her foot at an over-eager sheep
dog,

Actions of patient defiance that can be repeated
From generation to generation
Whenever the situation recurs:
Be in touch therefore with your extremities so that words
Can fall from your hands and feet as well as your lips
Be a quiet gymnast let meaning shine
Out of your person like light from a lamp.

Seriousness is all to the good but learning
In the academic sense is useless
And so is the body-building correspondence course
You take yourself as you are
As naked as you were born
And learn to steer the soft machine in flight
As if you were a stone skimming on water
Where the tide is time and each time you touch it
You are able to leap and sing.

A Rural Man

A rural man. His battered hat shading his eyes
He opens his gate. On any day of the year he looks wise.

His work is incomplete. It never stops.
If he grins he grins at the sky not at the crops.

He has a wife. She does what she has to do. That river flows
Without his help. He stares and everything grows.

What signs does he read? What formulae
In woodsmoke? How hard does he try

To conjure out of imperfect fields a perfect farm
Behind those fibrous weeds an ideal form?

Meanwhile, in this space, unconcerned with infection, he
                                        spits
And under the hedge, unencumbered by time and place, he
                                        shits.

At the Memorial

We remember wartime
Wartime
The leaves were red
Columns
Backs
Silences
Were broken
And skies were tight

Singers in uniform
Were frozen
Stony men
Were children
Nights
Flesh
Steel
Cracked burst buckled
Nothing was
The Target
Nowhere
The Retreat

We managed
The living the key workers
The throats of loyal trumpets
The minds of washed out cockpits
Our prayers were pistons
We managed
Our leaders in bunkers

As indestructible as rats
The tongues and necks
Of true survivors

In one cold wood
A headless boy
Still walks
A thin man prays
In his own blood
The dead
On every side
Wait to be counted

Catalogues
Printed
In old blood

Old wars
Are not doors
They are the walls
Of empty tombs
Bowed to
At stated times
By true survivors
Only dreams
Have hinges.

Branwen's Starling

I

The sun was on his side
    The wind set fair, the sea
A cradle that would break
    A fall, while tirelessly

That clown among the birds
    Flew looking for respect
And under his warm wing
    The painful letter kept.

That lesson that he learnt
    Before the kitchen fire,
Perched on the kneading trough,
    Now part of his attire.

The woman's fingers worked,
    Her face a sorrowing mask;
Her skilful stitching bound
    His body to his task.

Alas! those gentle hands
    That once were smooth and kissed,
Cramped and captive, scarred
    Like the two hands of Christ.

His burden is her woe,
    Her sighs must cross the sea
Under the starling's wing,
    A sister's misery.

2

That day he started out
　　As swiftly as a glance,
Rising above the Tower,
　　He had no second chance.

Was it the hour before dawn,
　　With frost thick on the grass,
Or moonlight or the stars
　　That saw it come to pass?

It must have been still dark
　　The day he left her hands
Before the morning bell
　　Awoke the warrior bands.

Before the chimney smoke
　　Announced the fires lit,
And brought the butcher boy
　　Yawning towards the gate.

Already like a stain
　　Across the unchanging sky
He saw the only course
　　Her tears would let him fly.

Let the cold sea stay green
　　And motionless as glass,
And let his seed of song
　　Grow in the wilderness.

Until the hermit sun
　　Emerges to display
Peaks and pyramids,
　　The monuments of day,

And, like a rousing shout
   After long silence, shine
The mountains into view,
   Cold water into wine.

3

Whatever time it took
   That journey from the earth
Into the nothingness
   Where myths are given birth,

The starling reached the land,
   He circled overhead
Where the shoreless seas
   Shrink to a river bed,

And searched among the throng
   Of figures in a field
For that one soul apart,
   A shoulder and a shield,

Like something sent from heaven
   To make the mighty wise.
He took him in his court,
   A giant for his prize.

One ruffle of his wing
   Brought her note to light,
But he had words as well
   To rehearse her plight,

How she was made to slave
   Above the kitchen fire,
Torn from her husband's love,
   Insulted in her bower.

Her sigh became his song,
    She taught him words, her name,
The message that he bore,
    That flight that earned his fame.

4

What happened to the bird
    The legend does not tell.
Did he return forthwith
    To the sad woman's cell.

Or sink exhausted there
    Unburdened, his abode
A grave upon the beach
    That Brân kneeled to prepare,

Or did he join the ship
    That led the vengeful fleet
Bound for the Irish shore,
And from the rigging call
    Each warrior at his oar?

The mast his stage, he plies
    Unruly parodies
A blackbird in the sails
    With thrush's melodies.

Their laughter never fails,
    Their smiles are bright like swords,
As though their world were free
    Of grief and tragedy.

Adapted from R. Williams Parry's *Drudwy Branwen*

Fragments from a Celebration

I

A bright bird lighted in the sheltered yard
Out of another sky and all his colours dazzled
Our native poultry. Above his head
There was consternation in the dovecote, the kind of fuss
You find among the well-fed and the tame.
The bright bird was unwise. He sang his own song
Unaccompanied, on a new scale
Without sympathy or support. Not so much wrong
As solitary. He was bound to fail.
That's you, my rejected friend. You were a fool
As for us, sound men of learning, we serve tea
While you serve time. The afternoon is on our side
Nothing disturbs our classic calm, no parish pump
Concerns. No echoing sighs. No prison cells.
We munch with precision our trimmed and buttered toast
You sew your mailbags for the General Post.

2

On our shoulders
Falls the day of defending
The day of twofold defence
The day of rebuilding our faith and preserving our frontier.
Beloved
The foundations of our world are giving way
Nearer and nearer through the eastern forests
I see the torches of the barbarians flicker
And in the African dust
The Vandal hordes swarm around the walls of Hippo . . .
And how shall we defend this city
On the day of defending

What dwelling place can we make
In brotherly love and vigilance
Unless we are one in Adam and one in Christ?
And in this lies the error of Pelagius;
He would break up the unity of man's nature
And break up our new unity in Grace
So that the man of learning and the ignorant man
Are no longer of the same stock, of the same nation
But each must conjure out of himself
His own selfish heaven
Complacent and self-satisfied
Even on the day that the Goth rides in.

3

The tramways climb from Merthyr to Dowlais
The slime of a snail on the mound of slag
This was once Cymru, now a dump
With cinemas derelict and rain on the barren tips.
The pawnbrokers have shut up shop: the labour exchange
Rules this dead land:
The face of the earth crawls with the last corruption:

My life is likewise, seconder to those motions
That move from committee to committee
To jack the old country back on its creaking feet:
Better maybe to stand on the corner in Tonypandy
Looking up the valley and down the valley
At a scattered wreck sinking in the mud of despair
Stand like a tip, men and rubble equally discarded.
We are already dead and our eyes are dust
We sucked the drugged waters of death in our mother's

milk

We cannot bleed as our forefathers bled

Or work with hands that have grown without thumbs:
When our feet are crushed in a fall
That makes it easier to bow in the free clinic
Raise a cap with respect to a wooden leg the insurance and
      Sir Alfred Mond's pension:
We are tamed. We no longer nurse a proud language or any
                resentment
And our gift to the world is a row of Labour M.P.'s.

4

But the wind turns. The early morning mist
Was scattered by the slow power of a royal sun.
There was a breadth of afternoon
And a sunset of streaming banners
Before the Great Bear closed his arms around the night sky.
There was a loading of carts in the cornfield
And in the orchard the dew glittered
On the still gossamer that hung between green apples.
This was Michael's gift, a hill to restore us,
A sanctuary of summer haze in late September
Before the winter, before the testing time, before the
                dark . . .

Michael, lover of mountains, pray in our hills.
Michael, friend of the maimed and the sick, remember
                Wales.

Adapted from lines by R. Williams Parry and Saunders Lewis

JOHN TRIPP

Ennui

I fork a fish finger
into my mouth, dip a chip
                    in tubed mustard.
On the box the clowns yelp
between the corsets and cat food.

Five minutes and I will be back
under the bedroom shelves
of Namier, Maitland and Bloch —
distancing myself, evading

private experience again. It is nice
there, the past in hard covers,
my thin life forced back
into history by some deep need.

Concerns

Such small ones, when I consider
the weight on family men
of carrying theirs.
Today, for instance, will see me
caring for an elderly aunt
who is visiting.
She is slow and deaf,
but proud and stubborn.
I would not reveal my concern
openly to her, yet I feel
we may not see her again.
I shall arrange a surprise
before she goes: a choice
of my late mother's millinery
and a sherry at the Park.
I wish my father would return
on the west train with her
to see Cornwall again.
He has lived here long,
but his home is there
and always has been.

I carry no pack on my back
and the days look smooth
in others' eyes. But these
small matters wrapped in silence,
these responsibilities of pity
can vex and nag. They seem
suitable candidates for concern.

The Icicles of Grief

– Well, that's that, my grandfather said.
The horses kicked up the slush
as the wagon pointed lifewards
again, back into the charades.
Traps bumped a score of kin
over wheel-ruts and potholes
to the house for sandwiches and tea.
Grandad took a swig from his flask.

Two miles away the old lady was bedded
after fifty years of dominion,
settled beneath a hedge of nettles
not far from the Ogilvy pit.

To me the matriarch was a ramrod
in bombazine, unsmiling always,
as if in perpetual mourning herself –
a source of acid-drops and pennies.

Probably it would take a week
for the loss of the familiar
to sink in. There was a drill
here, the discipline of dry eyes.

Later I would learn to hear
the thunder of reserve, come to know
our squirm at the mention of death.
But that day I was unprepared.

Now, through our black ritual,
the horses clopped to the entry

in a flurry of snow and the veils
lifting from the white faces.

Such restraint, I remember, their lips
sewn. Not a solitary tear
dabbed by the women as they glided
in whispers, and the sheepish men
anxious to be gone. How odd
I thought even then, that soon we slip
back under our masks, and button-up tight
our pain behind the black apparel.

Thin Red Line

In this little school on the moor
I think the teacher is making a last
stand. Undefeated, she ushers me
to her hopeless group, not to be reached
by poetry in this granite block
at ten of a sodden morning.
Introduction is made: the stale visitor
chugging up the coast to analyse a page
of Auden, or to read my own guilt.
They whisper and giggle, only stay quiet
when I shout lines like a barker
at a fair ... Then it is over, we take
weak tea and say nothing. We both know
we are outnumbered, keeping a flag flying.

Headmaster

Now, thirty years on, I shift
nervously in respect, perhaps slur
my speech on the tavern court.
He is still formidable.

Under his arm is the fat
original Gibbon in faded red boards,
savoured with a wall-length stock
at his widower's villa.

He has a stick, and his limbs
are frailed and bent, but the awed clock
could stop in his Star Chamber
long back when he told me

I could amount to something, or
nothing. How many callow bluecoats
passed his window into the grey
mixer beyond? He saw them run

towards it, without literature
or history. Sometimes I think
his kind of iced wisdom is best –
the goodness of sad reason.

Fidgeting there, trying hard to account
for the locust, my chronicle bulges
to impress him. As I skulk off,
his example makes it seem nothing.

Dismissal

To this day I remember
that alcove: flaked coffee-coloured
paint, an ashtray spilling, two
vodkas. As she broke it
with one sentence, I remember looking
left at an old lady
pouring her stout. Funny,
how at turning-points and news of grief
we do the ordinary. 'Oh,'
I said, as if my little finger
had been cut. It was more
embarrassment than shock. Three years
it took for her words to sink in.

Night Sorting in Victoria

When I finish one A-to-Z pile
another sack spills on the bench,
emptied by a silent man with a crooked smile.
Envelopes for Stoke and Bethesda,
thin packets to foreign parts
flip into pigeon-holes,
thumb and finger flicking them
like dealing cards. A long line of men
shoot good and bad news into slots.

Under powerful striplamps
the big room hums with trolleys,
a racket of whistling drivers
                                loading on the ramp,
            and shouting postmen
throwing parcels marked Fragile.
The old 'surgeon' in a glass box
tries to sellotape a ruined package –
a tube of Smarties lies open on the floor.
The fast sorters with snooker-hall pallors
                        work at twice our own speed,
slotting the envelopes in a buff-and-white blur.
The interest of a thousand addresses
and the race against the clock
combine to kill boredom.
At midnight we knock off for supper.

It goes on like this until dawn,
clearing the stacked bulging bags
till the last one has gone.
Then a floorwalker nods his approval
and a chargirl brings round the tea.

My wrist aches from eight hours
of sending letters on their way,
my eyes prick from squinting at scrawls.
Sorters droop along the line
like rowers after a boat race;
even the whistlers have stopped.
Half-asleep
          askew in a corner
          with the other lost bundles
I hear the first train rattle out,
see through a high grimy window
the first light creep down a winter sky.

A David Jones Mural at Llanthony

for Jeremy Hooker

I

Rain had turned the countryside
into a sump. From Capel-y-ffin
that constant, dripping screen obscured the hills,
drowning a file of ramblers
and swallowing two sad pony-treks.
I sheltered under sopping oaks,
then lifted a latch into a long
monk's larder, with boxes of bad apples, oranges,
mouldy biscuits and cake,
a mysterious pyramid of fresh eggs.
On the stone lay a splintered carafe
crusting a sediment of wine at the base.

Then I saw it . . .

Delighted, I remember thinking:
if the dealers receive wind of this
they'll climb here with mallet and chisel.
It was a signed
original, flaking fast on a cracked wall –
the dark buff and faded red of his fine
leaning script, the numerals of Rome,
a Christian head and a believer's praise embedded in the
text.
Time and neglect were chipping at beauty, scraping a
masterpiece.

(He had walked this corridor,
studied the portraits of Tudor marytrs,

put his brushes on the floor beside me,
and gazed at the Black Mountains.
A few days, fifty years before,
occupied his mind and hand
to leave us a lost symbol
like some flourish of hope.
   Feeling, wondering, testing, watching,
   seeing clues in fragments –
   '*For it is easy to miss Him at the turn of a civilisation.*')

2

Six winters from the Flanders mud
he came here, looking for a slot
of peace, some method to preserve sanity.
Deep reticence after misadventure
informed his plan; the chronicles that unlocked his horror
were yet to be written.
                         All that complexity,
the full bulging yield of myth
was growing as he painted on a monastery wall –
history to be sacked, language to be made,
the honours far off, and the life
continuing, aimed at the past.
Its price brought the long
loneliness, to be lived through in a Harrow room,
for one soldier of goodness and truth.

At Bosherston Ponds

Near the ancient village of Bosherston on the south Pembroke
coast, the lily ponds are so old that no one has been able to fix
the date of their forming.

In November it is desolate, and distant
from the ruck of summer. The mashed carpet of leaves
lie apple-rust in the gravegaps,
their season done. Waves of high grass
wash about the church, drowning
the sunk mounds, the lopsided slabs
askew from weather and dying stock.
Names illegible beneath layered moss
clip me to futility, yet give that mild
pleasure we feel in cemeteries.
I am cousined to them by nothing
but a moment in Wales
and the loom of skulled union
under roof of turf with the winning maggot.

History on this dot of the map
is sufficient to make me limp
a foot high. In my pocket a poem
shrivels to pinpoint. I look backward
for the peglegs hobbling
while I walk in cold time. I slither down
a long path mucked to a whirl of dung
and hang onto branches for support.

                              Solitary now
on a balsa bridge across the lily ponds,
I lose all strut.
Skidding along slotted planks, the bridge shakes

as my flimsy tenure shakes. I look out
at sheer rock and sloped dune, stretches
of water lily: something perfect occurred here
long ago, hacked in silence
without men or words – gaunt-winter-perfect
in frame of steel . . .

                         I turn back
up the steep track of churned cattle mud
where dead anglers trod, full of their hooked skill,
and riders stumbled, chasing a streak of vermin.

                       I scramble up
to slap of sea wind in my face
howling through the lost cemetery.
To the bang of winter, the coming events –
and the illusion of action.

Notes on the Way to the Block

There's a good crowd here today
to see me off.
I never knew I had so many friends
or enemies. I see several
familiar faces, and breasts.
There's one *cariad* smiling
whose knickers I took off
long ago in West Tredegar.
I don't see anyone crying.

Well, now to get down
off this bloody cart.
A few in the crowd
give me a helping hand,
eager to speed my departure.
Nice of them. I never knew
I had so many friends.

The sun is shining
but the birds have gone.
Birds can sense a bad scene.
The crowd is silent, a bit awed
but looking forward to the experience.
I mount the steps, alone,
see from the corner of my eye
the executioner approach
wearing a jester's cap and bells.
Good. We don't want black
or melancholy at a time like this.

His axe looks sharp.
I give him a cigar to make it clean and quick.

Don't I get a last request
like a joint or a slug of whisky?

Someone in the crowd giggles,
but I can hear one woman weeping.
I take a last look at the sky.

cariad = darling

Tomcat

While others were curled on their evening rugs
or purring on laps to a loving stroke,
this one was loosening dustbin-lids
to get at the fish-heads. With a rattle and crash
he'd dive in to select the garbage.

We say we like cats for their coldness,
seeing in their chill the slow dignity
we wish we possessed – no messy affection there,
nothing of slop to bring a rift
between Tom and his lessons in reality.

We had a blackbird family in a laurel hedge.
He waited on the wall for treacherous dusk,
squeezed through the branches and murdered the mother
and chicks. We saw the red feathered remnant, scattered
in a raging minute from life to gobbling death.

Those like him that lope in predatory dark
are men's men, criminals looting on the run.
If they see a hot cat on a roof, sex is the second choice
to a guzzling kill. His ancestors lived on farms,
the equal of anything vicious on four fast legs.

His history was probably short, a panther thrown out
from a series of heaving litters
stinking in a barnyard of cat orgy –
his mother and brothers drowned in a shuttered barrel.
Flung in a ditch, he began with grass-high vision.

He stared at the battlefield, grew bigger on mouse and
sparrow,

checked the competition and liked what he saw.
No pamper of milk came to soften him,
human hands were to spit and bite at.
When he arrived in our garden, his pessimism was quite
complete.

No one ever called him pussy, except old ladies
fuddled in sentiment. A black scavenging scrag,
for a month he shocked birds from the lanes,
rummaging wherever a stench was pleasing
and lodging on a sack in a shed.

There they found him, asleep, and clubbed him to a pulp.
He wouldn't taste full cream now, or caviare from tins.
Lean aloof prowler, he deserved no catafalque.
But after they threw him in a pit, I put him on a spade
and buried him under a scarecrow hanging in the wind.

Welsh Terrier

for Fay

Taffy of course. He would be called that,
our family being dangerously original.
He came as a mischievous black-and-tan ruff
from some Vale farm, affection leaking from him
in a coddling house. We had our work cut out
keeping him within his breed's toughness,
this ancient hunter of otter and fox.

Above the spoiling he kept himself hard,
brave in terrible scuffles with vicious strays
resentful of his clean line, dark vindictive curs
with wolf fangs. Scars and stitches grooved
his wire-wool head. With brisk rump and back legs
firm against attack, his great humorous whiskers
grinned at a world full of romp and forage.

Sometimes, over the shagged mountain
for three days he was missing on a bitch
jubilee. These roaming strumpets liked him
for his talent of tenacious pursuit
and rough satisfaction. In the mud lanes and farms
around Rudry and Machen, a few mongrels still trot
the wide district of their father's pleasure.

As he grew older his timing went, the small body
a lumbering cart, feeling the January edge
in bitter snowfields. Not even he, old loyal bruiser,
grizzled on twinge and cramp of age,
was fit to see the light of day. We
trickled brandy into him and mopped
his dry mouth with a cloth for a week.

We only heard him growl once, like an old man,
when his last ruined blanket was removed.

Badger

Harmless they call him, a lovable nocturnal thing,
a family man spending daylight in his deep sett.
He has an old reputation for remaining aloof.
I thought he stuffed himself on insects and roots,
a fallen egg, a few mice, nothing his own size.
But from a cable-drum he came sniffing for our buck
after dark, baiting him and scratching at the mesh,
then deadly serious one night with his big jaws
and his bone-crushing molars rampant.
He wanted much more than a boring vegetable dish.

Grizzled snouter with the claws and thick white stripe,
he scooped a hole under the boxwood hutch,
splintered the floor with his ramming head
and then clambered up and through it.
Our poor young rabbit must have died of fright
but not before the badger minced him
into string and red slippery pulp.
That lovable thing left a smear of blood and droppings
on a mile-long strip of hutch and run
before a smallholder blew his head off.

Stackpole Quay

A scavenger mole now, grot and sea-ruck
in this cold snow wind where brief family pulp
litters the stirred pebble. The summer's gone over the hill.

Down there at the buffeted, butting slab
swung long rusted grapplers for hooking
bounced smacks to the wall, the phased flotillas of fish.
                          Toppled captains brought slippery
portions of mackerel in. Good grizzled captains salt-
                                        whacked,
trawler-buried, all carried down to the sea mist.

Airfield

Flung down between useless scrub and good farm marl,
it sits there like some patrician folly
nobody wants, unmarked on maps,
with one riddled windsock, dented oil-drums and a few
rotted chocks, old sand seeping from bags
on the gun emplacements. Foul-stench Nissens
shudder in the whistling gusts, are for lovers
displaced at night, and the snouting

                             weasel, stoat and rat.

Invincible nettle and weed are cracking
the concrete open, a sagging hangar
rattles under shreds of camouflage net.

Seeing it, I think of the brash squadrons
bundled off to their dates
in that festival of turbulence,
the posthumous gongs and citations
for an élite of valorous wings.
Would I be here but for that kind
of fealty to a striped flag
blasting the Breton pens and Baltic
rocket shops in a cortège of wrecked metal?
Who now in this cenotaph silence
can give them a late benediction,
or say the last paternoster?

Disraeli at Llandaff

Under the window his small chipped head
is carved in stone. My overnight bag
replaces his portmanteau in the brown room.
An ostler freshened the horse
before a brougham whisked him in a loop
to the ruffed Widow Lewis at Greenmeadow.

The shoppers in the village street
do not mark the odd carving.
From here the bright Jew paid suit
to his Welsh lady, sharp and chockful
of charm over drumsticks and lemon tea.
The great house buzzed with importance.

That famous beak and black goatee
are left in split stone. This room
enclosed the bane of Peel
and Gladstone, hob-nobber with Khedive
and Empress, the wit who trimmed
through bloat of dull transaction.

Below, tucked in their own hour,
the shoppers pass the mouldered carving.

Famous Man

The devoted plasterer and his mate
on a plank between two ladders
fixed the blue plaque to a wall.
It tells me that he lived there
and gives the dates of his span.

What it doesn't tell me is where
he was born, the narrow street
that put pity and steel into him
in equal quantities. The tub-thumper
drumming up support for justice,

mesmerising the poor on corners
and bulleting through the council
to Westminster. How the people
loved him, and would have followed
his mind and his heart to millennium.

The proud plaque of Wedgwood blue
doesn't say how he spent
too many hours in turncoat lobbies,
in dark-suited trimming clubs
or in week-end boxes by the river

where love of the game for its own sake
is all. Why his soul got crusted
with shit on the long way up
and the short way down. And what happened
after power riddled him like pox.

Scott Fitzgerald in Hollywood

It wasn't this side of paradise.
The hooked mogul squinted at the script
and told him they couldn't shoot adjectives.
Neat gin was the solver in Beverley Hills
when the skids were greased.
He propped up the sham bar
in a place called the Garden of Allah,
framing those perfect sentences
that would never see the light of print.
His dazzle through the reckless twenties
spluttered in a sink of pap.

The crack-up letters tell a story
of art bending to the wind:
a wife in long shock, a daughter scared,
the bad famine of his gift.
He felt that God might have kept
his shop open, or Lenin. He left
those chiselled fiction structures,
redeeming his evening of waste.
He died alone in the dream factory,
forgotten by most,
unfinished like his last tycoon.

On Location

When we reached Barafundle
the script was still being mangled
by the director. His kind of thickness
took years to develop.
We parked the two caravans
on the clifftop, and the girl
gave us cheese crusts and Bovril.
The three actors sulked among the sheep.

A disaster of lost celluloid,
a few thin talents wasted away
kicking heels in the sea tussock
and clamping mud. The camera jammed
while the director did his Visconti,
having orgasms over coastal light.
I watched the life of a dead poet
disappear on perishable film.

At dusk we packed up, beaten
by temperamental gadgets, foul weather
and moods. I flung the soggy script
into a hedge, joining the black tantrum.
The church clock tinnily struck six,
all the sensible sheep stared at us,
and gulls floated in merriment
and the sea laughed on the sands.

Dewi Emrys

Vagabond with a taste for wine and people,
he took four chairs and a crown,
then pawned the crown in Swansea for a couple of notes.
He slept under paper on the beggars' benches
and in Cardigan barns, glad of a crust of bread
or a ladle from the churn. On street corners
through a screen of rain you might see him
hitch up his collar beneath the dripping troughs.

He should have been a cocky troubador
stepping from tavern to tavern
with his slung lute, singing for his supper.
Our century could find no home for his heart.
What trouble takes a man of skill and vision
to the skidding edge? A wayfarer like all of us
but haunted, he journeyed from a warm centre
high in the bright pavilion of bards

to the lost shabby rim.
I think of him when he was alone
with only a pen and a gaping page,
facing an old language with humility,
testing the sounds, turning and turning the lines,
drumming their response through his head.
He sits with Dylan in that narrow room
where the lyric is measured, sealed and folded

into himself, where the craft is always stubborn.
I saw him once in a smoky distance
outside his nest at Talgarreg, sweeping the leaves.
He wore an old fisherman's hat and a leather jerkin,
seeming peaceful at last within that silent frame.

The moss is over him now, the briar and ivy.
His mark is a perfect quill and a brimming jug,
a short poem shaped like a heart.

Chronicle of Two

Matt's hinge was the Old Testament.
Upon this he hung his bludgeon
to defeat iniquity wherever it thrived.
Twice a week he addressed the Temperance
and scourged women who were known to be loose.
His only vice was an evening cigar.
Crusty, chilling and deaf, he renounced his sons
as they tumbled into secular posts,
resisting his brimstone religion.

Emma was the shuffling crone in his bed,
graceless and one of a stock of strays
long-beaked and hard. Sixty-five years
went to her cold forming. She blinked
behind double lenses, snuffled
in alcoves, flicked dusters with her stub
yellow hand, sucked butterscotch
and padded about the house of blinds,
belted drapes and locked portholes.

Daylight faded as soon as it began
when the preacher rapped on the door.
He and Matt played a solemn game
of besting each other at biblical texts,
quoting chunks of Judges and Kings.
Their ransack of memory scraped through the night
as Emma nibbled duck in the kitchen
and threw bones to the hound,
making cocoa for the men when Matt rang a bell.

To break the boredom of sullen days,
she trapped mice in the larder, kept them,

then roasted them on the stove alive.
Matt complained of this oddness, but gave her
latitude for a helpless streak.
About her was a permanent odour
of Monday's wash. Her mouth puckered shut
like the drawstring of a mustard bag
if I asked for an errand's shilling.

One Sabbath in a snowy winter,
Matt was humming a few bars of Pantycelyn
when she sagged in the amber lounge.
He reached for his layman's cloth
in a throbbing requiem tribute
for the woman we thought was his wife.
We saw how the coldest affection is missed
when it's gone. Soon he followed her, intestate,
whispering a passage from the Covenant.

Among the Skyscrapers

Dylan Thomas in New York

Here the grocer and the moneylender,
the pushing pens of the revenue,
couldn't reach him. He was safe
from bills and wife, if not from living.

He could have earned a thousand dollars
for his cabaret act round the bars –
standing the language on its head
with that fag hanging from his lip.

Imagine the evenings, the crescent of fans
and followers, waiting for the measured spill
of words in that swirling smoke,
lines of wet tumbler rings on the wood.

In amber haze the jugnights ran
with cryptic wit and sonorous whimsy;
he turned a cold shoulder to no man.
Here his great spirit stopped twitching.

Then later the moment on the sidewalk
as rain fell, the back-slappers dissolving
into their own lives. Suddenly
the old black factor, chill of aloneness.

Badly wanting evidence of heaven,
he performed beyond the bugling call
of any bard's duty, and died from shock:
'I have seen the gates of hell,' he whispered,

'and it's a long, long way from Swansea.'

The Gnarled Bard Undergoes Fame

I

It is laughable really: three decades
of drought, pie-crust flung to me
like a dog at the metropolitan feast.
Behind shutters in the damp west
I weaved patchwork that resembled vision.

Now the rodneys come, to a hermit-crab with pad
and ballpoint, contraptions to frame my expression
and every move, supposing my cracked lips
utter truth or a white panacea.
They chase rainbows through my skull.

Wine is flowed for me, with rump beef
in the best crumbling hotel: suddenly
the landlord looks up, greasing his finger
for something he doesn't comprehend.
England brings glamour with her queens.

Clanking ferocious, in winter doldrum,
I manage a stiletto smile for the scribbling
beaver, a few icicles of logic
hissed at the modish don.
They lap it up like cats on the cream.

Perhaps they lick some prospect
of farce, my joining the cram of explosive
wit, with the lyrical child who died
in the heartless skyscrapers. But I am not
given to splendour; my brief is spare.

2

Wales bleats through its sheep in the corners
of sodden fields, their sackcloth shepherd
limps home to his tumbledown wreck. How
can I tell these shiny gropers of the long
fortitude that went to our making?
(Ancient fuss, the reason may be on their side
as the globe shrivels. Engines drum
above me, on their way to slicing
the barriers. Europe looms like a fat egg.
Yet still I walk to the sheep's pasture.)

The young sometimes stroll to my boots
with dignity, holding their own crimson banner
aloft. Scags of longing for ripeness
rip my album, my old chronicle wilts
under heat of enterprise.
Slip back the thread a notch or two
and the rust shows. Between country, love,
and the grasp of a psalm, slow pillage
loots the soul. Now the rodneys slide
through my bramble for a heavenly word.

I could hobble to the rim of this province
and jump off, my loneliness and I
sinking among the silent fish.
But I shall wait for tomorrow, when the noise
has gone, and I may listen again to the wind.

rodneys = undesirables

Turner in Old Age

I

Remote, cantankerous and fat
little man, hermit-mossed and solitary,
he slipped all the hollow connections
his fame could have brought.

Odd shylock in retreat, his bleak ways
spread rumour of madness.
At Chelsea he locked his spirit
behind the screen of his landlady.

Praise was heaped, yet he festered
at those barbs of 'suds and whitewash',
the dauber with a dripping brush
soaked in a bucket of ochre.

Puny man was swallowed by his canvas,
crumpling before nature, the brief split-
second of his span dissolving
against time, and its companion, light:

Yellow flame at morning, crimson
shockbursts of noon, an orange glow
sunk behind a ruined city;
rainbow shafts flooding through glass.

What he glimpsed was a passing
of empire, vainglorious shreds
at sunset, an edifice toppling
in broken masonry. The deluge.

Gondolas prowl through lagoons
between palaces that already sag,
their tapestry mildewed and flaked
like those ramshackle fallacies of hope.

2

Soured and gout-worn, he hid
from green calumny, dismayed by men,
by steam and speed slicing through nature.
Disgust drove him deeper into his hole.

It seemed as if life itself
was only a space to cram
the red and golden blaze of paint
across those distant horizons.

Like a haunting outside the frame
of day, the images from history
darken and clamp. For a moment the light
splinters, usurped by drumcloud.

Still he pieced that concept of something
lost and beyond us, a splash and streak
of sun and water fusing, the huge
melancholy of shaping a vision.

What it cost built his rack
and achievement, that stuns us now
as we look. An explosive mixing of pigments
made a radiance of mystery.

Down to the very end he sealed
his meaning: 'You cannot ever

read me, and do not care. Let it all
pass; go your ways.'

And then, as bent custom would have it,
they laid the painter in St Paul's –
one skull that had seen the pure value of light,
the fleeting whirlwind of light . . .

Henry Signs

The blaze of gold quartering
is caught in a sun flood through the high window
flashing all ways at once.
Ancestors slabbed in marble on the walls,
pearl, brocade and scarlet lions
jumping in the lemon shafts.
The living Holbein portrait hoists
himself and his precious cod-piece
off his ulcered calves,
thinking of bed and backgammon.
Lee and Cromwell and a creep of courtiers,
a slither of damp bishops
ease to the long table.
The pale black secretary dips the quill
and hands it to the ruin:
this once Golden Hope of the New Learning
soon to queen again
as easy as he split from Rome,
and now with levity pocketing
the hapless land to the west.
Sun-slant catches his enormous
ring-seal as he lifts his ruffed whiskers,
shakes white lawn sleeves
back from his wrists, scratches slowly
on buff parchment, and impresses red wax
with the ring, screwing it left and right
thoroughly for four hundred years.

A Note from Plwmp

With a name like that
we had to stop. It conjured pictures
of fat friendly shopkeepers
and comfortable landladies, gossiping in Welsh.
True enough, they gave us bacon sandwiches
and tea for two florins.
Around the corner a student
hot from Aber was painting road-signs.

I looked at this piece of Wales –
old, hospitable, rebellious
still weaving the lingo on a taut loom
they kept to a bardic codicil
boxed and clean on the shelf of speech.
Down south it dropped like a fart
at Elizabeth's table, as strange as English
in Sebastopol. It cut like a lost lament
through the flat twang of merchants.

Only a gull's flight from Mersey
they stitch this lexicon,
laying new pages and mending the old.
That student had a brave new pluck:
he risked Judge Jeffreys and the cold assize,
the grey wigs who push a plainsong
back down the throat.

We left little Plwmp like pilgrims
who had just seen Jordan,
knowing the sea dawns would break
over the language of Cardigan.

Testimony

Democracy
is a rattle on the doorstep
at seven in the morning
and you know it's the milkman.

One Sunday we were sleeping with our wives
when who should rap on our door
but the secret police from Shrewsbury.
We refused to talk to them in English
so they sent to Bala for handcuffs
and two interpreters.
We cooked them a breakfast of eggs
and sat around the kitchen in silence.
I gave one of them a copy of the Bible (in Welsh)
and he handed me a union jack.
They charged us at noon with sedition
and drove us to Swansea gaol.

As I write my memoirs in a cell,
I think of arrest and trial,
the rational content of law
and the democratic process.
I wish we could find isolation,
dignified peasants without a Tsar.
                                    Like the Russians
vilified and huddled together,
making our own mistakes,
giving two cold fingers to the world.

Commitment

Through a long fallow month, I could envy
the love-men, naturalists, land -
scapers, and diggers for old bones.

This chronicle I did not choose
stays tardy, and fails to give up another
missing piece. I sink to a dabbler.

The blinds are drawn, and the rain
spatters on the glass as I fiddle
with an elegy. That step I know so well

will not be heard tonight. To this
I have grown accustomed, yet linger
as if keeping vigil. So be it.

Capital

This will be the last ditch to fall
to the swing of its country.
Significance blowing down the hills
dies on the wind. Here the puffed
clink in their chains of office,
and the hagglers squat like a junta.

It is still as separate as an arm
lopped from its body: a strange sleeve
of territory spilled across the border.
What time has so carelessly mixed
clots here, where the ideals sag
and roots sprout only on the surface.

As long as I remember, the droll warmth
of its people has blurred
when our flag is lifted. Mouths are stitched.
Nothing is put to close scrutiny;
a knotted topic is flicked
into the bin, with a grin for Wales.

But now, in the distance, I think I hear
the young villagers build our future,
laying the first bricks of change.
This capital means less to them
than the land, where everything stems.
'Wait,' they are saying. 'Wait for us.'

A Kind of Penance

Unscraping to an ermine clique,
none of my kin brushed a catafalque
with soldiers bowed at the corners
and crowds to pay homage.

Swinging knapsacks to a shaft
they booted it, some bandily from a stoop
in a low seam. Unlike the film
they never sang on the road to the pit.

Near forty years on, their waste
sticks like a burr on my spirit
and will not loosen. Uncharity
drifts even to friends. Who are these

I watch now at the soft coffee-hour,
seeming all-in-all to themselves?
We are padded through the kind hours
at such distance from our crippled stock.

Unfair, the dealer's haphazard spray
that sends men to deep dark
and others capering in light.
Their portion of history drums at the mind.

Loss shrivels enterprise to a dot:
some things I latched to significance
– dignity and worth beyond price –
slip their eminence and become like the dead.

One day, clear as a black marker,
the lost ghost that relates to nothing
must show itself. All those deaths
shape my own defeat. It is inescapable.

Bards

In places where the language is spoken
   they dissolve into the people,
asking for no pompous rank
   or red carpet to their doors.
Sometimes a cap is doffed
   to one who has reached an eminence
of years and chairs of honour.
   I remember an old lady who said:
'I see Mr Llewelyn has died.
   I didn't know he was a poet.'
Fame for them is a tarnished bauble at best.

   (The narrowness can eke itself
into living: a small place brings its own
   horror to the sensitive, when drip of trivia
bolts him behind his limited tongue.)

   Parson, teacher, tailor, clerk,
in rooms with the candles guttering
   they wrote what they felt and saw
on pages that may always be lost
   on the outside world. Yet there are two
or three who would hold their skill
   with Europe's paragons.
For more than a thousand years
   their role has not changed,
nor would they wish it to plant them
   apart from their fertile soil.

Where the Rainbow Ends

to Sam: Gilfach Goch, March '74

My companion points to his cradle
in this gutted bowl of moorland scrub,
the slopes bravely greened
                 and won from the black alps.
A crater tombstone a community,
           its heart ripped out.
My mind's eye sees his father
lift again from shallow pitwater
for the climb home, the thick black tea
and cheese, the cold eating him.

It is a blue spring dusk
as we enter the terraced loop
             above the gutted place,
with grass thrusting from slag by a fake waterfall.
The machinery has gone for scrap,
leaving a huge silent coffin.

The scooped past lies at our bootcaps,
and our people and their ways
               gone with it.
    Down the valley
the stack-flares shoot like blowtorches,
the rattle of panic output
pricing men back into the market.

In the brittle kick of a moment's
accomplishment – this mind I sell for money –
nothing acts like the valley's balance.
Away from the rickety cardboard struts

I feel a slider, diminished always
by yesterday's story. What dreams of kin
broke here beneath the ash? Nice sentiment
wears a lid, and gentility vanishes
with the layers of charm and grace.
God still hides in the useless tin-shack chapel.

My companion looks at the bedrock
of his nurture, the running hopes
of his beginning, on the sheeptrack mountain
                    that once belonged to him
where tomorrow blew free as the wind . . .

Too old to forget, too proud
of stiff lineage to disown it,
we follow the bramble and rusted wire
out of yesterday – back to our customs
in the empty warmth that smothers
                                    what we have lost.

MORE ABOUT PENGUINS
AND PELICANS

Penguinews, which appears every month, contains details of all the new books issued by Penguins as they are published. From time to time it is supplemented by *Penguins in Print*, which is our complete list of almost 5,000 titles.

A specimen copy of *Penguinews* will be sent to you free on request. Please write to Dept EP, Penguin Books Ltd, Harmondsworth, Middlesex, for your copy.

In the U.S.A.: For a complete list of books available from Penguins in the United States write to Dept CS, Penguin Books, 625 Madison Avenue, New York, New York 10022.

In Canada: For a complete list of books available from Penguins in Canada write to Penguin Books Canada Ltd, 2801 John Street, Markham, Ontario L3R 1B4.

PENGUIN MODERN POETS

Penguin Modern Poets is a series designed to introduce contemporary poetry to the general reader by publishing representative work by each of three modern poets in a single volume. In each case the selection has been made to illustrate the poet's characteristics in style and form.

Some volumes in the Penguin Modern Poets:

POET TO POET

The response of one poet to the work of another can be doubly illuminating. In each volume of this new Penguin series a modern poet presents his own edition of the work of a British or American poet of the past. By their choice of poet, by their selection of verses, and by the personal and critical reactions they express in their introductions, the poets of today thus provide an intriguing insight into themselves and their own work whilst reviving interest in poetry they have particularly admired.

Already published:

Crabbe by C. Day Lewis
Henryson by Hugh MacDiarmid
George Herbert by W. H. Auden
Ben Jonson by Thom Gunn
Pope by Peter Levi
Shelley by Kathleen Raine
Tennyson by Kingsley Amis
Whitman by Robert Creeley
Wordsworth by Lawrence Durrell

Future volumes will include:

Arnold by Stephen Spender
Keats by Ian Hamilton
Marvell by William Empson
Swinburne by I. A. Richards